THE DUKAANDAAR MINDSET

Why India's Small Businesses Think Bigger Than Startups

PRATEEK JAIN

STARDOM BOOKS

www.StardomBooks.com

STARDOM BOOKS
112 Bordeaux Ct.
Coppell, TX 75019, USA

FIRST EDITION JUNE 2026

STARDOM BOOKS, LLC.
112 Bordeaux Ct. Coppell, TX 75019, USA

www.stardombooks.com

Stardom Books
United States and India

THE DUKAANDAAR MINDSET

Why India's Small Businesses Think Bigger Than Startups

PRATEEK JAIN

p. 150
cm. 13.97 X 21.59

Category : BUS025000 – BUSINESS & ECONOMICS / Entrepreneurship
SEL031000 – SELF-HELP / Personal Growth / Success
FAM012000 – FAMILY & RELATIONSHIPS / General
BUS041000 – BUSINESS & ECONOMICS / Workplace Culture

ISBN : 979-8-950206-00-9

Dedication

This book is dedicated to my father and Mother, the people who never stood on a stage, yet taught me everything about business, dignity, and life from behind a shop counter.

To the countless hours they spent building something from nothing, to the silent sacrifices no one applauded, and to the values they passed on without ever calling them lessons.

It is also dedicated to every *dukaandaar* who has ever been underestimated,

every second-generation entrepreneur who has felt the weight of expectations, and every individual standing between tradition and transformation, trying to build something of their own.

This journey began in a small shop, but it was never small in what it taught me.

And finally, to anyone who has ever questioned their path, felt unseen, or wondered if they could build something bigger This story is for you.

Acknowledgments

Writing this book has been a journey of reflection, honesty, and acceptance. While the story may carry my name, it is built on the presence, influence, and support of many people who shaped me along the way.

First and foremost, I am deeply grateful to my father. Everything I understand about business, resilience, and dignity began with watching him stand behind a counter every single day. He never taught through lectures, but through actions, discipline, and consistency. Whatever I have built is rooted in the foundation he created.

To my mother, thank you for being my emotional anchor. In moments of doubt, frustration, and uncertainty, your calm belief gave me the strength to continue. Your simple words often carried more clarity than any strategy ever could.

To my family, thank you for your patience and trust. The journey of building something is never easy on those around you. Your support allowed me to stay focused, even when the path was unclear.

To every customer who walked into my shop, you gave me more than business. You gave me lessons, trust, and the opportunity to grow. Each interaction shaped my understanding of value, relationships, and responsibility.

To my vendors and partners, thank you for your belief and continued support. In an industry built on trust, your confidence in me helped me move forward, especially in the early days when I was still proving myself.

To my early team members and colleagues, thank you for standing by me during uncertain times. Building something from the ground up requires people who are willing to believe before results are visible. Your contribution has been a part of this journey.

To those who doubted me, rejected me, or told me I wouldn't succeed, thank you. Your words stayed with me and became a source of drive. They pushed me to stay, to improve, and to prove through work, not arguments.

To the mentors, teachers, and individuals I encountered along the way, knowingly or unknowingly, you added perspective to my thinking. Every conversation, every disagreement, and every experience contributed to my growth.

And finally, to the reader, thank you for picking up this book. Your time, attention, and openness mean more than you realize. This story becomes complete only when it connects with yours.

This book is not just an acknowledgment of people; it is an acknowledgment of a journey that was never mine alone.

Contents

Introduction

I did not learn my first business lesson in an MBA classroom. I learned it standing behind a shop counter, watching my father negotiate with a vendor over a cup of tea. I did not know it then, but those simple moments were preparing me for a journey that would stretch far beyond the four walls of our shop. Long before I knew what leadership meant, I saw it in my father's quiet confidence. Long before I understood the word "operations," I watched it unfold in every bill, every return, and every stock check. Long before I dreamed of becoming an entrepreneur, a shop counter became my first window into the world.

Growing up behind a counter is a different kind of early education. It teaches you to listen before you speak. It teaches you to observe people. It teaches you the value of relationships. It teaches you that trust is built not through speeches but through consistency. It teaches you that business is not just about products but about people, conversations, habits, and emotions. I did not know then that these small lessons would one day become the foundation of a book. I only knew that life had placed me somewhere uncommon, and that I had to understand why.

For years, I carried questions inside me that I did not have the vocabulary or courage to articulate. What does it mean to inherit something you did not create? How do you build on a legacy without breaking away from its roots? How do you take a shop into a future filled with algorithms, apps, and instant gratification? And most importantly, how do you find your identity when the world has already decided who you are?

Whenever I spoke to people who came from family businesses, I realized they carried the same invisible weight. We shared the same guilt, the same doubts, the same contradictions, the same pride, and the same pressure. Some of us were called lucky because we inherited a running business. But no one saw the emotional burden that came with it. Others were told we had it easy. But no one understood the responsibility that came with the opportunity. Over time, I realized something important. Second-generation entrepreneurs do not inherit just a business. They inherit expectations. They inherit history. They inherit habits and systems created long before they understood the meaning of change. And somewhere between all this, they also inherit silence.

That silence is what pushed me to write this book.

I reached a point in my life where the journey felt bigger than the shop. Not because I had achieved everything, but because I finally understood the story behind why I stayed. I wrote this book because I met countless others like me. People who were trying to modernize a business that the world assumed was outdated. People who were battling the generational gap, not because they lacked ambition, but because they lacked acceptance. People who wanted to innovate but felt guilty about disturbing the familiar rhythm their parents had built. People who wanted to build something new without disrespecting what already existed. People who wanted to take their business from "dukaandaar" to "corporate" but did not know where to start or how to justify the journey.

This book is for them.

This book is for the second-generation entrepreneur who feels torn between tradition and transformation. It is for the young man or woman standing behind a counter, wondering if they have it in them to build something bigger. It is for the shopkeeper who feels underestimated, the startup dreamer who feels confused, the family member who feels unseen, and the quiet leader who has ideas but no one to discuss them with. It is for the fathers raising the next generation and the sons and daughters trying to understand their place in the legacy. It is for every person who has hesitated to call themselves an entrepreneur because society has made the word sound more glamorous than the reality they live in.

But this book is not a manual. It will not give you a checklist for revenue or a formula for funding. It is not a hundred hacks to grow faster. It is not a step-by-step guide on becoming a unicorn, nor is it a guarantee that reading this will change your business overnight. This book is not about shortcuts or secrets. It is simply a mirror. A mirror that reflects the journey of someone who started from a place most people misunderstand. A mirror that shows you that your doubts, fears, struggles, and dreams are valid. A mirror that reminds you that being a shopkeeper is not small and being an entrepreneur is not exclusive. A mirror that tells you that both identities can belong to you at the same time.

If you are looking for a how-to playbook, this is not it. But if you have ever said to yourself, "Me too," then you will find yourself in these pages. Because this is a story built on honesty and clarity, not formulas. It is a story about failing, learning, rebuilding, rethinking, breaking myths, and rising again. It is a story about discovering that dignity and ambition can coexist. That tradition and innovation can stand side by side. That the shopkeeper and the entrepreneur are not opposites, but extensions of the same identity.

What this book offers is not advice. It offers perspective. It offers stories that shaped my thinking and may shape yours.

It offers the mindset shifts that helped me grow from reacting to the world to responding to it. It offers lessons I learned the hard way, so you may recognize them before they cost you time or confidence. It offers truths that we rarely speak about. It offers reflections that might make you pause, breathe, and rethink the way you look at your business or yourself. And it offers permission — permission to grow in your own way, at your own pace, without feeling the need to fit into the world's definition of success.

The journey you will read about in the chapters ahead begins where most business stories do not. It begins in a shop. In childhood memories of dusting shelves, counting coins, sorting inventory, and observing customers. It begins with identity. It moves into the clash between "dukaandaar" and "entrepreneur." It explores the fear that quick commerce created for thousands of local businesses. It reveals how traditional setups can borrow lessons from corporate systems to become stronger and more organized. It looks at fathers and founders standing on opposite sides of the same idea. It explains how branding is not decoration but clarity. It highlights the people behind the scenes who make every shop function. It touches on the emotional struggles of a second-generation entrepreneur who appears confident on the outside but carries silent battles within. And it moves toward strategy, clarity, and intentional growth. By the end, the story circles back to its purpose and the reason this book exists.

If you are reading this, I want you to know something clearly. You are not alone. You are not the only one juggling legacy and innovation. You are not the only one who feels the pressure of expectations from family, society, and yourself. You are not the only one who wonders if you are doing justice to what you inherited or what you want to create. You are not the only one who has been misunderstood for coming from a family business.

You are not the only one who has felt guilty for wanting to modernize something that has existed for decades. You are not the only one struggling with comparison, whether with startup founders, corporate professionals, or the generation before you. You are not the only one learning how to lead while learning who you are.

This book is my story, but I hope it becomes a space where you find your own story reflected. It is written with the simple intention of telling the truth. Not the glamorous truth the internet likes, but the quiet truth most of us live. The truth of small beginnings. The truth of disruptions that shake you. The truth of generational conflict. The truth of the pride and pain of carrying a legacy. The truth of learning to think strategically after years of survival. The truth of mistakes that become turning points. The truth of people who stand by you. The truth of growth that is not always visible. The truth of becoming a leader even before you call yourself one.

As you turn these pages, I invite you to walk beside me through the journey. You may not relate to every detail, but you may recognize the emotions behind them. You may not run a shop, but you may understand what it feels like to inherit a path you did not choose. You may not face my challenges, but you may see your own reflected in them. And somewhere along the way, I hope you find clarity, courage, or even comfort.

I wrote this book not to teach, but to connect. Not to instruct, but to include. Not to preach, but to share. Because stories have power. Stories make us feel seen. Stories remind us that we are part of something larger. And stories help us rewrite our own.

So, before you begin Chapter One, let me say this. Thank you. Thank you for picking up this book. Thank you for giving space to a story that started behind a counter. Thank you for being open to seeing your own journey within mine.

I hope these pages give you a sense of direction. I hope they make you feel less alone. I hope they challenge the myths you have carried. I hope they help you take one brave step forward. And I hope they inspire you to write your own story, not someday, but soon.

This book is my story. But it becomes complete only when it meets yours.

CHAPTER 1

Born Behind the Counter

MY PLAYGROUND WAS NOT a park filled with swings or slides. It was the shop floor. While other kids my age were playing with cricket bats, remote-control cars, or video games, I found myself surrounded by ledgers, spare parts, and conversations that revolved around margins, credit, and trust. The smell of grease and the sound of shutters opening each morning were as familiar to me as the sound of a school bell.

I often say I didn't learn my first business lesson in an MBA classroom. I learned it standing behind a shop counter, watching my father negotiate with a vendor over a cup of tea. There was no textbook, no PowerPoint, no professor, just the real-world give and take of business, played out in a small shop.

I was born and raised in Delhi, a city that itself feels like a bustling marketplace, where survival depends on hustle and connections. My schooling was in Delhi, and like many middle-class children, I was told early on that education was my ticket to a secure future. I worked hard, studied harder, and eventually earned my MBA from IMT Nagpur, followed by an executive program in Kolkata. By then, I thought I was firmly on the "professional" path, the one where you dress in crisp formals, carry a laptop bag, and measure success by designations and appraisals.

And for a short while, I lived that life. I worked in the corporate world at a large, structured, and methodical organization. I had a desk, a team, and a predictable monthly salary. In fact, I was even on the verge of a promotion. On paper, it all looked perfect. My family felt proud. My friends saw me as "settled." I should have been content.

But I wasn't.

Inside, I felt a restlessness I couldn't shake off. I realized that while the corporate environment gave me stability, it didn't give me excitement. I craved risk. I wanted to test myself in situations where the outcome wasn't guaranteed, where my decisions had direct consequences. In the corporate setup, there were too many buffers. No matter how much effort I put in, the results were diffused across layers of processes, approvals, and hierarchies. That predictability, which was comforting for many, was suffocating for me.

By 2016, the thought of continuing like this became unbearable. I was in my mid-twenties, young enough to take a leap and old enough to realize the cost of inaction. I often tell people that 2016 was my rebirth, the year I truly began my entrepreneurial journey. I decided I couldn't keep waiting for the "perfect" idea or the "perfect" timing. If I wanted to do something of my own, I had to begin.

But begin where? That was the bigger question. I spent months searching, reading, and brainstorming. Every idea I looked at seemed either too far-fetched, too capital-heavy, or too far removed from my interests. My heart kept asking me to build, but my mind reminded me of reality: I couldn't afford endless trial and error.

During this confusing phase, I naturally turned to my father. He had been in business for years, running a modest automobile spare parts shop in Delhi. It wasn't flashy, it wasn't "startup material," and frankly, I didn't feel inspired by it. The automobile spare parts industry was unorganized, chaotic, and full of inefficiencies. It didn't have the glamour of fintech, e-commerce, or technology-driven ventures that everyone in my MBA circle was chasing. In fact, compared to the polished image of corporate offices, stepping into that world felt like a downgrade.

I can admit this now; I was hesitant. I looked at the shop and thought, *"Is this really where my MBA degree is going to land me? A tiny counter in a dusty market?"* For someone who had just come out of a structured corporate setup, it felt like diving into disorder.

But life doesn't always follow our carefully crafted plans. Destiny has its own way of nudging us into places we're meant to be. My conversations with my father began as casual discussions but soon turned serious. He told me, *"If you want to start something of your own, why not begin here? You have a background, you have some understanding, and you'll at least have a foundation to build on."*

At first, his suggestion felt disappointing, almost disheartening. I had dreamed of building something shiny and new. Yet, the more I thought about it, the more it made sense. Every business, no matter how small or unglamorous, was still a business. And if I could learn to succeed in an unorganized, chaotic space like this, perhaps I could succeed anywhere.

After weeks of debating with myself, I made the decision. I left my job. I turned down the promotion I had been waiting for. And I stepped into the world I had resisted, the automobile spare parts business.

It wasn't a grand launch. There was no ribbon-cutting ceremony or media coverage. It was simply me, standing in a small, dusty shop in Gurgaon, sweeping the floor, arranging shelves, and waiting for the first customer to walk in. That was the true beginning of my journey. And though I didn't realize it then, that little step, leaving the comfort of a predictable salary to embrace the uncertainty of a shop floor, would shape the entrepreneur I was destined to become.

The Humbling Start

It was hardly the kind of beginning most MBA graduates dream about. After years of studying management, sitting in lecture halls filled with strategy case studies, and preparing PowerPoint decks on how to scale billion-dollar companies, I found myself in a cramped 300-square-foot shop, tucked beside a noisy garage in Gurgaon. That little space became my first "office."

There was nothing glamorous about it. My workplace had a single counter that doubled as my desk, one old chair, and a fan that barely managed to push hot air around. There was no air-conditioning, no automated shutter, no staff to delegate tasks to, and certainly no boardroom filled with colleagues in formal suits. It was just me, a few shelves, and the faint smell of oil and rubber from the garages nearby.

Every morning, I would leave home in East Delhi and embark on a two-and-a-half-hour commute. It wasn't a smooth drive in a company cab; it was a combination of metro rides, bus changes, and long walks. By the time I reached the shop, I was already exhausted, but I had no option. The Gurgaon markets opened early, and I had to be there before the first mechanic or customer came looking for parts.

My ritual began the same way each day. At 9 AM, I would roll up the heavy shutter. It wasn't automatic; it was one of those old iron shutters that groaned as they opened, as if mocking my inexperience. Some mornings, the shutter would jam, and I would stand there struggling, sweat dripping down my forehead. On more than one occasion, I had to call out to nearby mechanics for help. They laughed about it, and I laughed with them, but deep down it reminded me how far I had fallen from the neat, polished corridors of corporate India.

Once the shutter was up, my first tasks were nothing like the responsibilities I had managed as a corporate executive. Instead of checking emails or preparing presentations, I swept the floor, wiped down the counter, and dusted the shelves. It wasn't optional; if I didn't clean, no one else would. After that came a small puja, a prayer ritual my family always believed in before starting business for the day. Lighting the incense stick in that dusty shop gave me a strange comfort, a reminder that even in chaos, tradition grounded me.

One morning, I snapped a photo of myself holding a broom and sent it to my former manager. Just a few months earlier, he had congratulated me on a corporate promotion I had turned down. His reply came quickly: "What progress!" It was laced with sarcasm, the kind that cut deeper than he probably intended. For a moment, I felt humiliated. I had left behind a stable salary, a career path, and an identity, only to find myself doing janitor's work in a dingy shop.

But as I look back today, I realize that was one of my proudest moments. Yes, it was humbling, but it was also liberating. I had chosen this harder path willingly, and because it was mine, I owned every bit of it, the good, the bad, and the uncomfortable.

The early days were brutal. Business was painfully slow. Some days, not a single customer walked through the door. I would sit behind the counter for hours, staring at the shelves, fiddling with ledgers, and wondering if I had made the worst mistake of my life. Time moved painfully slowly when there was no work to do. Every evening, I carried that frustration home, and more than once, I vented to my mother.

I told her I felt trapped in a dead-end. *"Papa has pushed me into this,"* I said bitterly. *"He made me leave a good job, and now I am stuck here."* It was the kind of frustration every entrepreneur goes through in the early days, the regret of stepping into uncertainty, the fear that maybe the leap was too big, the worry that you've gambled away your best chance at security.

But my mother, in her calm way, reminded me of something simple yet profound: *"Every seed takes time to sprout."* Those words have stayed with me ever since. Growth isn't immediate. Just because nothing seems to be happening on the surface doesn't mean something isn't taking root underneath.

In hindsight, those early days were my real MBA. They taught me patience, resilience, and humility. They stripped away the ego that often comes with a degree and a corporate title. They forced me to understand that entrepreneurship is not about glamour; it's about grit. Success doesn't arrive overnight, and often it looks like failure at first.

Standing in that dusty shop, broom in hand, I began to learn the hardest truth of entrepreneurship: before you can build, you must be willing to start small, embrace discomfort, and endure the silence of empty days.

The First Sale That Changed Everything

Every entrepreneur remembers their first customer. It's not about the size of the order or the amount of profit; it's about that magical moment when an idea becomes real because someone else believes in you. For me, that moment arrived in the form of a young man, no more than twenty-one years old, who walked into my small shop one afternoon.

He was looking for a spare part for his Chevrolet Beat, a car that wasn't very common at the time. His father had recently gifted it to him, and as any young driver would, he wanted to get it back on the road quickly after a small repair. By sheer luck, I happened to have that exact part in stock. When I pulled it from the shelf and handed it over, I could see the relief on his face. For him, it was just a car part. For me, it was so much more.

That sale, small in monetary terms, felt monumental. It was my first real transaction, the first tangible proof that I could run this business. The rush of excitement I felt as he paid and left the shop is hard to describe. It wasn't about the money at all; it was about validation.

After weeks of waiting in an empty shop, doubting my decision, and second-guessing myself, here was evidence that I could actually create value for someone. Someone had trusted me to solve a problem.

A few days later, his father came to the shop. He told me his son had said my store was the only place he could find that particular part. What struck me more was the story behind it. He explained that he had given the car to his son not just as a gift, but so that the family, especially his wife and elderly mother, could travel comfortably. The spare part wasn't just about fixing a car. It was about ensuring the family's mobility, their independence, and their peace of mind.

That conversation changed me. Up until then, I had been treating the shop as a place where I sold automobile parts. That day, I realized I wasn't in the business of selling metal and rubber. I was in the business of solving problems that mattered to people. For that family, a working car meant weekend outings, trips to the doctor, and the simple comfort of not being stranded.

The part was small, but the impact was big. It shifted my mindset completely. I stopped seeing myself as *"just running a shop."* Instead, I began to view my role as someone creating value, contributing to people's lives in ways I hadn't recognized before. That pride became fuel.

Entrepreneurship is often described in grand terms, such as innovation, disruption, and scaling. But at its heart, it begins with something much simpler: solving one person's problem better than they expected. My first sale taught me that. It gave me the conviction that even in an unorganized, chaotic industry, I could build something meaningful.

That young man probably doesn't even remember me today. But I remember him, because he unknowingly gave me my first real proof of purpose.

Lessons From the Shop Floor

Those early years behind the counter taught me more than any MBA program ever could. Don't get me wrong, my MBA gave me frameworks, vocabulary, and exposure. But the shop floor gave me reality. It stripped away the jargon and forced me to face problems head-on, without the safety net of a corporate system.

Running a shop meant I had to be a one-man army. In a corporate office, responsibilities are neatly divided: HR handles hiring and policies, finance manages accounts, operations manages processes, sales drives revenue, and marketing builds visibility. But in my shop, all of those roles collapsed into one, me.

If a customer walked in, I was the sales manager. If the stock was running low, I was procuring. If a vendor needed payment, I was the finance person. If the shelves were dirty, I was the housekeeper. If an assistant didn't show up, I was HR. There was no department to escalate to, no manager to delegate to, no colleague to cover for me. The shop demanded that I wear multiple hats every single day.

At first, I found this overwhelming. It felt like I was juggling a dozen balls in the air, terrified of dropping even one. But over time, I realized that this experience was shaping me into something my MBA couldn't, a hands-on entrepreneur who understood every cog in the business wheel.

The Hidden MBA of Shopkeeping

The world often underestimates shopkeepers. The word *dukaandaar* is used casually, almost dismissively, as though it means "someone small" or "someone ordinary." Yet, the sheer breadth of skills required to run even a small shop is immense. If you pay attention, a shop is nothing less than a business school for life. Every transaction is a lesson in negotiation. I learned to sense hesitation in a customer's tone, read body language, and hold my ground without losing the relationship.

Unlike corporate negotiations, where people hide behind contracts and email trails, these were face-to-face, real-time deals. One wrong word, and you could lose both the sale and the customer's trust. Every customer interaction is a crash course in psychology. Some walked in confident, already knowing what they wanted. Others were confused, anxious, or even angry. I had to adapt instantly, to reassure, to educate, or sometimes just to listen. These micro-interactions taught me empathy in a way no leadership workshop could.

And every delayed payment was a test of resilience. Vendors wanted their dues on time, but customers often delayed theirs. Cash flow was always tight, margins were razor-thin, and every rupee mattered. I had to learn patience without losing firmness, and diplomacy without compromising discipline.

Over the years, I began to joke, half-seriously, that shopkeepers are the most underrated CEOs. They don't wear suits or sit in glass cabins, but they run operations, manage risks, and keep cash flowing, often with far fewer resources than a startup founder with venture capital.

Think about it. A CEO is judged on vision, execution, and sustainability. A shopkeeper delivers all three every single day. They forecast demand based on customer habits, manage supply chains through relationships, and balance books with ruthless efficiency. Unlike corporate CEOs, they don't have the luxury of burning cash for years before turning a profit. Their survival depends on staying cash-positive every day.

And perhaps the biggest difference is that they operate under the radar of respect. Society may idolize startup founders, but the local *dukaandaar* quietly embodies entrepreneurial spirit in its rawest form.

My father was my biggest teacher in this regard. He was not educated in management theories, but his instincts were sharper than any strategy document. He had one principle he drilled into me again and again:

"If things are not working, don't blame the market or the world. Look at yourself first."

At first, those words felt harsh. I wanted to blame circumstances. I wanted to say customers didn't understand, vendors weren't reliable, or the industry was unorganized. But his advice forced me to take ownership. It made me ask: *What could I do differently? Where did I fall short? How could I adapt?*

That mindset shaped me deeply. It made me accountable and self-driven. It also gave me confidence. Because if the problem was within me, so was the solution.

One of the most valuable skills the shop taught me was anticipation. In the corporate world, forecasts are made using spreadsheets, graphs, and algorithms. In the shop, I had to forecast based on observed behavior. Which parts were being requested more frequently? Which customers were likely to come back in a week? Which suppliers had the longest lead times?

Slowly, I developed an instinct. I could predict what customers would ask for before they opened their mouths. I could sense which vendors would delay deliveries and prepare alternatives in advance. These instincts became a survival tool because in our business, delays could mean losing not just one sale but a customer for life.

Another lesson was the power of relationships. In an unorganized industry, supply was not just about money. It was about trust. Vendors had to believe you would pay them on time, even if you asked for extended credit. Customers had to feel that you cared about their problem, not just their wallet.

I realized early that repeat business wasn't won by discounts; it was won by dependability. If someone knew that coming to my shop would save them time, effort, and worry, they would return. And when they returned, they often brought others along.

Word of mouth became my most powerful marketing tool, long before I thought about branding or advertising.

Perhaps the greatest lesson the shop floor gave me was humility. Nothing humbles you faster than sweeping your own floor after spending lakhs on an MBA. Nothing grounds you more than being judged not by your degrees but by your ability to solve a customer's problem on the spot.

There were days I felt invisible, reduced to just another shopkeeper in the eyes of society. But those were also the days that built my grit. They reminded me that dignity does not come from titles, but from the integrity with which you do your work.

In later years, when I began leading larger teams, I realized how valuable those early lessons were. Because I had done the work myself, the stocking, the selling, the cleaning, the bookkeeping, I could empathize with anyone I managed. When I asked someone to do a task, I knew the challenges they would face, because I had faced them too.

This gave me credibility as a leader. People didn't see me as someone who only gave instructions; they saw me as someone who had walked the same path. Leadership, I learned, isn't about commanding from above. It's about serving alongside, earning respect through shared struggle and shared wins.

Looking back, I often smile when I hear people talk about "entrepreneurial training" programs or expensive leadership courses. I respect them; they have their place. But I also know that the best MBA program in the world exists right in our neighborhoods, behind the shutters of small shops.

Every shopkeeper is unknowingly doing case studies every day. Every dispute with a customer is a lesson in conflict management. Every stock shortage is a crash course in supply chain optimization. Every delayed payment is a financial management workshop.

Ironically, society looks down on *dukaandaars* when in reality, they embody entrepreneurship in its purest form, resourcefulness, adaptability, persistence, and vision.

Growing up as a shopkeeper's son came with a strange mix of emotions, emotions I didn't always know how to process as a child. On some days, I felt immense pride in my father. I admired his discipline, his work ethic, and the way he carried himself with dignity, no matter how hard the circumstances. But on other days, especially when I was surrounded by my peers, I couldn't help but feel a tinge of embarrassment.

I studied at a well-known school in Delhi, one of those places where appearances mattered more than anyone would openly admit. Many of my classmates came from affluent families. They arrived in chauffeur-driven cars, often dropped off in sleek sedans with tinted windows. I, on the other hand, usually came by bike or by bus. While they carried the latest gadgets or branded shoes, I carried a simple bag and wore the kind of uniform that was "just enough."

As a child, comparisons are inevitable. You don't yet have the maturity to value struggle or sacrifice. What you see is what you measure yourself against. And in those moments, I felt the sting of being "different." I envied my friends' comfort, their shiny toys, and their ability to talk about foreign vacations or expensive hobbies. There were times when I wished my father were anything but a shopkeeper, because in the eyes of the world, that title didn't carry much prestige.

Yet, those feelings of embarrassment were always balanced, and often overpowered, by moments of great pride. Every evening, I would see my father return home, exhausted but never defeated. He worked long hours, standing behind a counter from morning till night, dealing with customers, suppliers, and sometimes unreasonable demands. And yet, he never complained.

There was a quiet dignity about him, a strength that came not from wealth but from resilience.

One day, when I was particularly upset about my situation, I voiced my frustration to him. I told him how unfair it felt to be compared with others; how difficult it was to constantly explain why we didn't have what they had. He listened patiently and then said something that has stayed with me forever:

"It doesn't matter how you were born. What matters is how you die. If you are born poor but die rich, people will remember you. If you are born rich and die rich, nobody will talk about you."

That single statement shifted something inside me. Until then, I had looked at life as a fixed equation: you were either born into comfort or condemned to struggle. But my father reframed it. He reminded me that birth is a chance, but death is a choice. Where you start may not be in your hands, but where you end up is shaped by your effort, your courage, and your decisions.

Over time, I realized he wasn't just teaching me about money. He was teaching me about respect. It's easy to envy those who seem to have everything handed to them, but that kind of respect is shallow; it belongs to their circumstances, not to their character. Real respect comes from creating something of your own, from rising despite the odds, from carving out an identity that no one can dismiss.

Looking back, I see that my father quietly embodied that philosophy. He may not have had the trappings of wealth, but he had earned every ounce of what he owned. His pride didn't come from comparing himself to others; it came from knowing he had built a life from scratch, with his own two hands.

As a boy, I often felt torn between pride and embarrassment. But as I grew older, I realized that both emotions were shaping me. The pride gave me strength. The embarrassment gave me hunger.

And together, they built in me a determination to prove myself, not to the world, not even to my peers, but to the standard my father had set: to live a life where respect is earned, not inherited.

That lesson, seeded in childhood, became the foundation of my entrepreneurial journey.

Responsibility Knocking Early

In 2016, just as I had made the decision to step away from my corporate career, life threw me a curveball. My father fell slightly unwell. It wasn't a major illness, but it was enough to shake me. For the first time, I saw clearly how fragile the business really was. Until then, I had thought of it as *his* shop, something he had built and managed for years, something that somehow ran on its own because of his discipline and effort. But when he couldn't be there, even briefly, the truth became glaringly obvious: if he stepped away, everything could collapse overnight.

That realization hit me harder than any management lecture or corporate training ever could. I suddenly understood the risks we had been living with all along. There was no formal structure, no second line of leadership, no backup plan. It was a one-man show, and that one man was my father. Being the only child, the responsibility naturally fell on me. There was no one else to step in, no one else to share the load.

In that moment, the business stopped being something I was "trying out" or "exploring." It became a lifeline, not just for me, but for my family. I knew I couldn't treat it casually anymore. If my father needed me, I had to be ready to shoulder everything.

That period stripped away any illusion of safety. There was no cushion, no fallback option. Unlike my corporate job, where a day off or a sick leave barely disrupted the system, here my presence was non-negotiable. I couldn't afford to fall sick myself, because if I did, the shop would remain shut and the cash flow would stop instantly. The weight of that responsibility was immense. Weekends disappeared. Holidays disappeared. The concept of "time off" became irrelevant. While my friends continued to plan trips, outings, and celebrations, I found myself anchored to the shop. From morning to night, my life revolved around shutters, shelves, and customers. At first, it felt suffocating. I missed the freedom that a fixed salary and structured environment had once given me. But as the days passed, something inside me began to change. With that burden came a new sense of ownership. The shop was no longer "my father's shop." It was mine to protect, mine to grow, and mine to prove myself through. Responsibility has a strange way of transforming your mindset. What once felt like a chore began to feel like a mission. I started looking at every detail more carefully, the way stock was arranged, the way customers were greeted, the way negotiations were handled. Every decision, however small, carried weight because I knew it reflected on me now.

That shift was subtle but powerful. For years, I had thought of myself as helping my father in *his* business. But in 2016, during those uncertain months, I truly stepped into the role of an entrepreneur. The shop became my test, my classroom, and my battleground.

Looking back, I see that period as a turning point. My father's brief illness was a reminder that businesses, like lives, are fragile if they depend on only one person. It also taught me something even more important: responsibility isn't a burden to be avoided; it's an opportunity to rise. That realization gave me strength and pride. From then on, I no longer introduced myself as someone who had "left a corporate job." I began to see myself as someone building a business of my own.

It was no longer about survival alone. It was about proving to myself that I could carry forward what my father had built, and perhaps even take it further.

Small Shop, Big Lessons

As the years passed, I began to understand just how valuable ground-level experience really is. My corporate job once gave me exposure to polished systems, well-defined reporting structures, and neatly documented processes. Those things certainly had their place. But the shop floor, raw, chaotic, and unforgiving, gave me something far more important: resilience, resourcefulness, and leadership in its truest sense.

Running a small shop forced me to sharpen skills I didn't even know I needed. In a corporate setup, you can rely on data, software, and teams to make sense of the numbers. On the shop floor, I had none of that. I had to learn to forecast demand simply by observing patterns, conversations, and customer behavior. I began to anticipate what customers might need weeks in advance. If a particular car model was becoming popular, I had to predict which parts would be in demand next. If I miscalculated, shelves sat full while cash flows dried up. If I anticipated correctly, I had customers thanking me for always having what they needed, exactly when they needed it.

Cash flow management became another hard-earned lesson. In the corporate world, budgets are approved annually, and finance departments act as a buffer. In the shop, there was no cushion. Every rupee counted. I learned to plan expenses with razor-sharp precision, to delay what wasn't essential, and to prioritize payments that kept relationships alive. Some days, I had to balance paying vendors and maintaining enough liquidity to manage day-to-day operations. Those decisions were stressful, but they gave me financial discipline that no spreadsheet exercise in business school could have taught.

Vendor relationships became the lifeblood of the business. In our industry, supply was not just about price. It was about trust. A vendor needed to believe that even if I asked for extended credit today, I would honor my word tomorrow. There were times when personal credibility mattered more than contracts. I realized that in a fragmented and unorganized industry, your reputation is your most valuable currency. That trust, once earned, often unlocked opportunities no amount of bargaining could.

But of all the lessons, the one that shaped me the most was humility. Nothing teaches you humility quite like sweeping your own shop floor while carrying an MBA degree in your pocket. It's a humbling reminder that education may open doors, but it does not exempt you from doing the hard, unglamorous work.

Humility also came in unexpected ways. I had customers who judged me not by my knowledge or qualifications but by my face, by the fact that I stood behind a counter in a small shop. Some looked at me dismissively, assuming I was "just another shopkeeper." At first, those moments stung. I wanted to tell them about my degree, my corporate experience, and the job offer I had walked away from. But soon I realized none of that mattered. What mattered was whether I could solve their problem. Respect in business is not demanded; it is earned, transaction by transaction, relationship by relationship.

Those experiences grounded me. They stripped away the illusions of status and prestige that often come with titles and degrees. They taught me that leadership is not about sitting in a corner office but about taking responsibility, no matter how small or menial the task.

Looking back, I see that the small shop was never really small. It was a vast classroom disguised as a counter and a shutter. It gave me lessons that would stay with me far longer than anything I learned in a lecture hall. Resilience, precision, trust, and humility, these were the true pillars of my education. And they were lessons I could only have learned by rolling up my sleeves and living them, day after day.

Misconceptions About Second-Generation Entrepreneurs

One of the things I have encountered repeatedly is the assumption that second-generation entrepreneurs have it easy. People look at you and think everything is handed down on a platter, the shop, the contacts, the business model, even the customers. On the surface, it may appear true. After all, you are stepping into a space that already exists, something your parents have built with years of effort. But the truth is far more complex than that neat picture.

Yes, a family business does give you a platform. You don't start completely from zero. You inherit some goodwill, some stability, and maybe even a bit of credibility in the industry's eyes. But what people fail to see is the baggage that comes with it. There are expectations, not only from family but also from society. There is constant comparison, the unspoken pressure to live up to your father's name, and the weight of not being the one to "spoil" what has been built. And perhaps the hardest part, the constant fear of being dismissed as someone who "just inherited."

That fear drove me for years. I knew that if I simply sat behind the same counter and ran things the same way, I would forever be seen as the shopkeeper's son, not an entrepreneur in my own right. I had to prove, first to myself and then to the world, that I wasn't just continuing my father's business. I was building something new, something bigger. The shop was my starting point, but I was determined it would never be my finish line.

Networking is another area where misconceptions run deep. People assume that because my father was already in the trade, I got easy access to suppliers and that doors automatically opened for me. The reality is different. Yes, his presence gave me a small head start. Maybe it shaved two or three years off the journey by making initial introductions a little smoother. But that was it. Beyond that, everything depended on me, how I conducted myself, how consistently I honored commitments, and how seriously I was taken as a professional in my own right.

Relationships in business don't survive on inheritance. They survive on trust and delivery. The respect I have from suppliers today wasn't inherited; it was earned, day after day, through actions, not lineage. If I delayed payments, it didn't matter whose son I was. If I failed to deliver value, no supplier would keep backing me. Very quickly, I realized that surnames might open a door once, but after that, it's your character and credibility that keep you in the room.

Being a second-generation entrepreneur is a paradox. On one hand, you are grateful for the foundation. On the other hand, you carry the constant burden of proving that you deserve to stand on it. And for me, that burden became fuel, fuel to push harder, to innovate, and to ensure that my journey would be defined not by what I inherited but by what I created.

The Evolution Begins

From 2016 to 2021, my life was defined by the shop floor. Those years were not glamorous and certainly not easy. Day after day, I opened the shutter, dealt with customers, balanced accounts, argued with suppliers, and tried to keep the wheels turning. There were times I wondered if all the effort was worth it, but slowly, brick by brick, something was being built.

By 2021, we had finally broken even. It may sound like a technical milestone, but for me, it was an emotional one. Breaking even meant survival, but more than that, it meant validation. It was proof that the long hours, the sacrifices, and the frustrations were not in vain. It was proof that I could sustain this business not just as a shopkeeper's son continuing a legacy, but as an entrepreneur in my own right. For the first time, I felt real confidence in what I was building.

That year, we took a bold step: we formally incorporated our company. Moving from an unregistered, traditional shop model into a structured company was not just a legal formality. It was symbolic. It meant that what began as a small counter with a single chair was now evolving into an organization with a vision and a future.

The physical space told the same story. What started as a cramped 500-square-foot shop slowly grew into multiple outlets. Each new space carried the same DNA of resilience, but each expansion also represented a bigger dream. We were no longer limited by geography or the four walls of one shop. We were beginning to imagine scale.

And then came the turning point, Jaipur. What had begun as a humble shop in Gurgaon eventually transformed into something that, at the time, felt almost unimaginable: India's first automobile mall. A 100,000-square-foot car mall that redefined how people looked at automobile retail. From dusty shelves and single counters to wide aisles and massive showrooms, the contrast couldn't have been greater.

Standing inside that mall for the first time, I couldn't help but think back to the boy who used to feel embarrassed about being a shopkeeper's son. The irony wasn't lost on me. What had once been a source of self-consciousness had now become my greatest pride. And the journey from that 500-square-foot shop to the 100,000-square-foot mall taught me something priceless: starting small is not a weakness.

In fact, starting small gave me an advantage. It gave me a foundation of grit and practical wisdom that no MBA case study could ever replicate. When you begin with nothing but your own hands and your own persistence, every step upward carries meaning. You learn to value every rupee, every customer, every relationship. You don't take success for granted, because you know what it feels like to sit in an empty shop for hours, waiting for a single sale.

The shop floor was my crucible. It burned away illusions and left behind resilience. It shaped my instincts, sharpened my decision-making, and gave me a sense of ownership that no classroom ever could. By the time we opened the automobile mall in Jaipur, I wasn't just celebrating an achievement; I was carrying with me the lessons of every struggle that had led up to it.

Looking back, I see those five years not as a delay or a struggle, but as the foundation. They were the years that transformed me from someone experimenting with business into someone committed to it. They were the years that turned my father's shop into my life's mission.

And as the business evolved, so did I.

Looking back, I realize that being "born behind the counter" shaped my identity as an entrepreneur in ways I could not have predicted. It gave me resilience. It gave me empathy. It gave me the ability to lead because I had done the work myself, from the ground up.

If you are a second-generation entrepreneur reading this, I want to tell you something: you're not alone. If you feel torn between pride and embarrassment, between tradition and ambition, know that it is part of the journey. You may have inherited a shop, but what you do with it is entirely your story.

A shop, if you pay attention, is the best business school in the world. Every day you stand behind the counter, you are learning negotiation, finance, operations, marketing, and leadership. You are being trained to run an empire, even if all you see today is a small shop.

Key Takeaways

- Growing up in the shop taught me the fundamentals of business long before any MBA classroom did.

- My corporate job gave me stability, but it never gave me excitement, ownership, or the thrill of taking real risks.

- Even though joining the family shop didn't feel glamorous, it became the foundation of everything I built later.

- What I initially saw as a limitation slowly revealed itself as my biggest strength.

- My entrepreneurial journey didn't start with a perfect idea. it started with restlessness and the courage to begin.

Chapter 2

Dukaandaar vs. Entrepreneur Breaking the Myth

"When I introduced myself *as a shopkeeper's son, people smiled politely. When I called myself an entrepreneur, they suddenly respected me more, even though I was doing the same work.*"

I have often wondered why society chooses its heroes the way it does. If you are a startup founder pitching on a stage with slides, a pitch deck, and a string of fancy terms, you are admired, even glorified. People lean in, they listen, they nod with approval. The same people, when introduced to a *dukaandaar,* react differently. If you are running a shop with systems, handling cash flow, juggling vendor relationships, and working with margins that are tighter than many MBA-led ventures could ever handle, you are dismissed. You are ordinary. You are called "just a shopkeeper."

I have lived this contradiction for years. I have been called both a shopkeeper and an entrepreneur, sometimes in the very same breath, and I have felt the sting of judgment as well as the quiet pride of proving people wrong. When I told people I was running a shop, their expressions changed. A trading business, spare parts, shopkeeping, these words did not go down well in my early years.

People looked at me with faces that said, "This is nothing." To them, trading was an easy fallback, something anyone could do. And yet, I knew that it was the very act of staying with it, of taking responsibility when things went wrong, of carrying the pressure of risk, of holding on to vision, that defined me as an entrepreneur.

The judgment came in many forms. Some believed family-run businesses were built on inheritance rather than effort. The stereotype was simple: you did not build it; it was handed to you by your parents. Others assumed shopkeepers made "wrong money," that profits in trade were somehow unearned or illegitimate. These are the perceptions I encountered again and again. For many, a shop was too small a canvas to paint ambition on. But for me, *Dukan* was where ambition met reality every single day.

It is easy to dismiss what you do not understand. Those who mocked shopkeeping never stood behind a counter when a customer demanded a solution on the spot. They never stayed awake, wondering how to balance credit extended to customers with payments owed to vendors. They never learned to build relationships where saying "no" was never an option. I remember my B2B customers in the early days, people like Mr. Varun and Mr. Pavan from Rod and Sierra Motors. They would remind me that in a local market, you cannot say no. If you do not have a product today, you can arrange it by tomorrow. That is the strength of local business. It is an art to say yes, even when resources are thin, to solve a problem before it becomes a complaint.

So when people judged me for being a dukaandaar, I reminded myself of what I knew from lived experience: this was not a lack of ambition. This was entrepreneurship in its rawest form. In fact, I often say that every entrepreneur should taste it — the ground level, the day-to-day running of a shop. Because it is here that you learn every department by doing. No MBA class, no textbook on KPIs or KRAs, can teach you what a shop counter can. You don't just learn finance, marketing, procurement, or logistics; you live them, simultaneously, all the time. That is the kind of education no one can hand you.

Still, the labels matter to the world. I have never been comfortable with them. Even today, when I see words like CEO or MD on profiles, I smile to myself. Which Dukan needs such titles? I have never used the word "entrepreneur" to describe myself. I remained a shopkeeper because the work mattered more than the title. And yet, I saw the change in how people treated me. When I called myself an entrepreneur, there was sudden respect. When I said I was a dukaandaar, the same work was looked down upon.

I have not forgotten the incidents that shaped this contradiction. There were emails from former employees who left me years ago, saying their time had been wasted because I was just a shopkeeper who would never build anything big. There was the professor in my marketing class during college who dismissed my ideas outright, telling me to choose a different career because I would not succeed in business. Those words stayed with me. I carried them until years later, when I returned to that same college as a guest lecturer, in marketing, of all subjects. I reminded the professor of what he had said, with a smile. It was not about revenge. It was about proving, through work, what words had once been denied.

And then there were moments on the other side, when being a dukaandaar gave me an edge. My first investor asked me how deep I was in my industry, what I knew that others did not. I answered from years of shopkeeping, from details only a person on the ground could know. That depth impressed him. That was when I realized: being a shopkeeper had equipped me with knowledge no pitch deck could replicate.

This is why I feel pride when I call myself a dukaandaar. Because it is not easy. It is not small. It is staying power. It is resilience. It is a substance. The myths that society attaches to the word are wrong.

And perhaps that is why I have made it my mission to break them.

This chapter is about that tension, about the myths that have been thrown at me, and about why I believe that "dukaandaari" is not a lack of ambition but perhaps the purest form of entrepreneurship.

The Weight of Judgment

In the early days, my business looked nothing like the glossy images of modern startups. It was unorganized, deeply traditional, and rooted in the trading of spare parts. To many outsiders, it seemed unimpressive. Trading, after all, is something "anyone can do." Or so they said.

When I told people I was running a shop, I could almost see their faces tighten with polite disdain. They were expecting perhaps that I would say I was joining a corporation, working in a fancy office, or building a tech company. Instead, I said I was running a trading business. A shopkeeper. That wasn't something they respected. To them, it was neither aspirational nor ambitious.

And yet, behind that single word, *trading*, was a world of complexity. There were risks every day. There were pressures I had to bear, both negative and positive. There was the uncertainty of cash flow, the constant negotiation with vendors, and the responsibility of making decisions that no one else could make for me. But none of this was visible to those who judged.

The truth is, the judgment stings. It stings because while others saw "nothing," I saw long hours of sweat, risk, negotiation, and persistence. They saw four walls and a counter; I saw the beginning of something that could grow. I was not just standing behind a counter; I was taking full ownership of every outcome, good or bad. If something went wrong, I knew it would be on me. If something went right, it was only because I stayed with it.

This is what many people don't understand. Entrepreneurship is not about looking big on day one. You cannot become big in one day. It takes years to build something worthwhile, and in those years, there are countless steps, failures, and restarts. Many people give up in between. That is why I always say: an entrepreneur becomes an entrepreneur only if he stays. To stay is to prove. To stay is to grow. And to stay, even when judged, is the real test.

But those early days were filled with reminders that what I was doing did not "count." I heard it in conversations. I saw it in people's expressions. Even silence carried judgment. For some, being a shopkeeper was a fallback, something you did when you couldn't do anything else. For others, it was a sign of lack of ambition, of choosing the easy way out. I lived through that perception, even though my reality was the opposite.

Running a shop was never easy. In fact, it was harder than most imagined. People thought starting a shop was simple. "Anyone can do it," they would say. They believed that a family-run business came with everything already prepared, that I simply had to show up. But when I stood behind the counter, I knew the truth. There was nothing automatic about it. Every relationship had to be built, every rupee had to be earned, and every decision had consequences.

I still remember the frustration of trying to build a team back then. Many people I approached dismissed me. *"You only run a shop,"* they thought, *"how can you build something bigger?"* Some even told me directly, *"You won't be able to do it."* Others left me midway, convinced that their time was being wasted. I still have those emails. They told me that I could never build a company from a shop. They judged before I could prove.

But that judgment, while painful, also became fuel. Every time someone underestimated me, I wrote it down. Every time someone said I couldn't do something, I remembered it. It gave me a zeal to prove through work, not words. People often say they don't work to prove others wrong. But I believe a little bit of that fire is important. It pushes you, especially when the world doesn't see your effort.

I recall even in college, during a marketing class, when I gave a different perspective on why the Tata Nano failed. The professor looked at me and said, *"What angle is this? Don't take marketing or business into your life. You will not succeed."* Those words cut deep at the time. But I carried them with me. Years later, when I returned as a guest lecturer at the same college, I spoke about marketing. That professor was present, and I reminded him of what he had told me. I said it with a smile, in a jolly way, not to put him down but to show how far I had come. That moment reminded me how much of my journey was about staying power, about continuing despite the judgments.

To the world, I was just a dukaandaar. To myself, I was learning the hardest, most practical lessons of entrepreneurship. I was building resilience, not reputation. I was creating value, even when others could not see it. And perhaps most importantly, I was proving to myself and to those who doubted that real entrepreneurship does not need society's validation. It needs patience, persistence, and the willingness to be judged while you quietly build.

That is why the judgment, though it stings, has never defined me. It is only noise. Behind the counter, beyond the stereotypes, was the reality of work that would one day grow into something bigger.

What Entrepreneurship Really Means

The irony is, from the very beginning, I always had a clear definition of entrepreneurship. It was never about swanky offices, big titles, or raising funding. Those things might impress society, but they never defined the essence for me. To me, entrepreneurship has always meant something simpler and much harder: being the one who takes risks, carries the pressure, and still holds on to a vision. That is the core. Risk, pressure, and vision. If you can handle all three, you can call yourself an entrepreneur. And it doesn't matter whether you are building an e-commerce platform or running a spare parts shop.

Over time, I have watched many around me chase the external markers of entrepreneurship, the designations, the photoshoots, the media attention. I've seen people use "founder" or "CEO" as badges of honor. But from the very first day of my journey, I understood that those things do not matter when the lights go off, and the crowd disperses. What matters is whether you can stay.

That word, "stay," is central to my definition. Anyone can start something. In fact, starting is the easiest part. Many even taste some success for a while. But an entrepreneur becomes an entrepreneur only if he stays. If he continues when enthusiasm fades. If he holds on through the failures, through the doubt, through the sleepless nights when everything feels like it might collapse.

I have seen this happen countless times. People start with big dreams, huge energy, and high confidence. But the first setback throws them off course. The first sign of struggle makes them quit. I have always believed that entrepreneurship is not about who shines the brightest at the start; it is about who endures the longest when the journey gets dark.

For me, this clarity came naturally. I accepted, from the beginning, that if something goes wrong, I am the one to blame. No excuses. No pointing fingers. Full ownership, full accountability. That mindset made me firm. It made me resilient. I could look at my failures without flinching because I knew they were mine to carry, just as any success would be mine to own.

This definition has not changed over the years. It has carried me through every high and low. When things went wrong, it reminded me that accountability is not optional.

When things went right, it reminded me that I had earned it through persistence. The balance of those two, failure without excuse and success without arrogance, became the rhythm of my journey.

This is also why I never felt insecure about being called a dukaandaar. People often use the word as if it were small, as if it lacked ambition. But I knew better. Because I understood that staying power, ownership, and risk-taking, these are the very traits that define an entrepreneur. And every shopkeeper, every so-called dukaandaar, lives those traits every single day.

A dukaandaar takes risks constantly. He decides what stock to buy without knowing how the market will respond. He extends credit to customers and prays they will repay. He negotiates with vendors, often staking his reputation more than his balance sheet. He bears the pressures —financial, emotional, operational—on his shoulders without complaint. And still, he wakes up every morning with a vision: that the shop will not only survive but also grow.

How is that different from the celebrated definition of entrepreneurship? The truth is, it is not. It is the same, only less glamorous. But substance has always mattered more to me than glamour. Titles are just labels. The real test of an entrepreneur is not in what he calls himself but in what he endures, what he builds, and how long he can stay on the path he chose.

I have always said that some things become possible only when you are firm about them and stay with them. Time itself moves you forward if you stay. But if you leave, time will leave you behind. That is why staying has been my mantra. It has been the difference between being judged as "just a shopkeeper" and proving, through persistence, that I am an entrepreneur in every sense of the word.

The Stereotypes We Face

Still, stereotypes cling. No matter how hard you work, no matter what results you produce, society has a way of reducing your story into a label. One of the most common stereotypes I faced was this: *"Family businesses are easy. Everything is handed to you on a platter."*

Nothing could be further from the truth. A family shop is not a cushioned inheritance; it is a responsibility, often a burden. When you inherit a shop, you inherit far more than a set of keys or an inventory list. You inherit expectations from your family, skepticism from society, and the heavy duty of carrying forward something that is not entirely yours, yet completely yours. It is a paradox: the business existed before you, and yet the moment you step into it, its future rests squarely on your shoulders.

This stereotype has followed me since the beginning. People assumed I had it easy, that my path was paved by my parents. They thought the business was already established, that customers, vendors, and networks came ready-made. But what they never saw was the countless hours of proving, of rebuilding, of reshaping something old into something new. In reality, you are not handed success in a family business; you are handed a responsibility that can crush you if you do not handle it well.

Another stereotype I encountered was about money. Many people believed shopkeepers made "easy money" or even "wrong money." There is an unspoken assumption that trading, by its very nature, must be dishonest, that dukaandaars cut corners, inflate prices, or somehow earn without effort. This perception is deeply embedded in society, and I have lived through its sting.

The truth, however, is starkly different. There is nothing easy about being a shopkeeper. To stand behind a counter every day and deal with customers face-to-face is not a job for the faint-hearted.

It requires you to handle complaints with patience, to balance credit and cash flow with precision, and to keep promises that stretch beyond numbers.

Margins in trading are razor-thin. One wrong move can wipe out your profit for the week. Every sale is a calculation, every transaction a balance between survival and growth. Vendors need to be managed, often with negotiations that test your patience and diplomacy. Relationships need to be nurtured because in a local market, trust is currency. Inventory needs to be tracked vigilantly because even one missing product can cost you a loyal customer.

People who dismiss shopkeeping have never lived a day of it. They have not faced the pressure of arranging a product overnight because a customer cannot be told "no." They have not understood how fragile a small business can be, and how much foresight it takes to keep it running smoothly.

What I have always found ironic is how the same qualities celebrated in startup founders are ignored in shopkeepers. Startups are applauded for risk-taking, for agility, for resilience. But these very traits are at the heart of dukandaari. A shopkeeper takes risks daily. He is agile by necessity, adjusting to market shifts without the luxury of large reserves. He is resilient because quitting is not an option; families depend on that shop, and communities rely on it.

And yet, despite all this, stereotypes persist. Family-run businesses are dismissed as unearned privilege, and shopkeepers are looked down upon as unambitious or even dishonest. But I have seen the opposite with my own eyes. The dukaandaar is often the hardest-working, the most grounded, and the most entrepreneurial figure in the ecosystem. He does not seek glory, but without him, commerce would collapse at the local level.

So, when I hear those stereotypes, I no longer get defensive. I know the truth. And the truth is this: Dukandaari is not about ease or shortcuts. It is about staying power, discipline, and the courage to carry responsibility every single day.

Lessons From Behind the Counter

The shop is a teacher like no other. It may not have air-conditioned classrooms, glossy slides, or professors with degrees, but it has the rawest form of business education anyone can receive. Running it gave me insights that no textbook could ever provide.

I still remember back in college, during my MBA, there was a program where we had student cooperative societies. One of the initiatives was a student-run restaurant. You could walk in, order a meal, and the entire operation, from supply to service to cash collection, was handled by students. I watched it closely, and it struck me that this setup was a small glimpse of what *dukandaari* looked like. But the difference was that I had been living this reality long before.

When I stood behind a counter in our shop, I wasn't just a shopkeeper. I was simultaneously the accountant, the salesman, the procurement officer, the customer service representative, and the logistics manager. A *dukaandaar* does not have the luxury of staying in a single domain. He has to run all the domains at once. Finance, sales, marketing, procurement, operations, everything passes through him. That is why I often say that every entrepreneur should spend time at the ground level.

In the MBA classroom, we were taught to define KRAs and track KPIs. They were introduced as abstract frameworks, something you would encounter once you moved into corporate life. But when you are running a shop, you don't just study KRAs and KPIs, you live them.

Every day you are measuring performance, adjusting roles, and tracking outcomes, even if you never use the jargon.

The reality is that theory often hides complexity. It makes you believe business can be neatly divided into departments and responsibilities. But the shop shows you otherwise. The boundaries blur. The shopkeeper has to handle everything, whether it is his "job description" or not. This is why, when people enter companies and are confined to one domain, they often struggle to see the bigger picture. But a shopkeeper never has that problem. His view is holistic because he is forced to operate across functions every single day. This is why I believe that without ground-level exposure, many entrepreneurs risk being fooled by illusions of scale, style, or structure. You might think your business is stable because your graphs look good or your presentation sounds sharp. But until you've been the one to explain a delay to an impatient customer, or scramble to arrange a product overnight because saying no is not an option, you haven't tasted the reality of business. The shop teaches you urgency. It teaches you humility. It teaches you that no matter how well you plan, execution lives in the messy, unpredictable present. Customers don't care about your strategy decks; they care about whether you can solve their problem today. And when you've lived that pressure, you acquire a grounding that no corporate training can match.

Pride in Being a Dukaandaar

The first time I truly felt proud of being a shopkeeper was on the day of my company's incorporation. It was a milestone, one that looked official on paper, but for me it carried something far deeper. That day, I realized that everything I had built up to that point, every instinct, every bit of resilience, every ounce of business sense, had its roots in the shop floor. Without being a dukaandaar first, I could never have become anything more.

It struck me with unusual clarity: the shop was not just my starting point; it was my foundation. The lessons I had absorbed behind that counter, by managing cash, handling vendors, and solving customer problems in real time, had become the building blocks of something larger. When I signed the incorporation papers, I understood that my identity as an entrepreneur was inseparable from my years as a shopkeeper. Far from being a handicap, dukandaari was my training ground, my edge.

That edge became visible in moments that could have gone either way. I remember the first time I pitched to an investor vividly. It was intimidating. Here was someone with capital, with choices, evaluating me not just for an idea but for credibility. He looked me in the eye and asked, *"What do you know about this industry? How deep are you in it?"*

It was a question that could unsettle anyone who had only read about markets in case studies or studied industries from a distance. But for me, the answer was instinctive. My depth came not from slides or reports but from years of living it. I could talk about customers by name, about vendors I had negotiated with, about patterns in demand that no report could capture. I could explain margins, risks, and opportunities not as theory but as lived reality.

In that moment, I realized that shopkeeping had given me something priceless, credibility born of experience. I didn't need to dress it up with jargon. The investor could sense the authenticity. That grounding was my edge, and I was proud of it.

Even today, when I meet shopkeepers, I feel a deep sense of solidarity and admiration. I know what it takes to stand behind a counter, to keep showing up day after day, to shoulder responsibility that few outsiders will ever recognize. Their work is invisible to many, but to those of us who have lived it, it is a mark of grit and resilience.

I often pause to observe them, the way they interact with customers, the speed with which they calculate margins, the instinct with which they read people and situations. These are skills that no MBA program or leadership seminar can replicate. They are born of ground reality, of staying power, of being in the trenches every single day.

On Labels and Titles

People often ask me why I don't call myself an entrepreneur. The truth is, I never did. I've always been comfortable with the word *dukaandaar.* Even when I see people introducing themselves with designations like MD or CEO, I can't help but smile. Which Dukaan really needs such titles? To me, the formality has always felt unnecessary, almost comical.

I never needed a label to feel secure about what I was doing. From the very beginning, I believed that work speaks louder than titles. The ability to stay with something, to carry risk and responsibility, to make decisions and live with the consequences, those are the things that matter. A designation on a business card cannot replace substance.

And yet, I've lived the irony of how the world reacts to words. When you say *dukaandaar,* people smile politely. It is the kind of smile that acknowledges you, but at the same time, quietly dismisses you. The word does not carry weight in conversations where ambition and aspiration are being measured. People hear "shopkeeper" and assume limits, as if your world can only stretch as far as your counter.

But when you say *entrepreneur,* the response is entirely different. The same people lean forward, listen more carefully, and even show admiration. It is the same work, the same effort, the same set of responsibilities, yet the world treats the two words very differently. The change is not in substance but in perception.

This difference has fascinated me over the years. Why does society glorify one word and dismiss another? Why does a startup founder automatically receive respect, while a shopkeeper has to fight for legitimacy? I've thought about it often, and I've concluded that it comes down to narrative. The entrepreneur is seen as building for the future, while the shopkeeper is assumed to be stuck in the past. But if you look closely, that assumption does not hold true.

Every shopkeeper I know is constantly adapting. He is reading markets, adjusting stock, negotiating credit, and handling competition. He is solving problems in real time daily. If that is not entrepreneurship, then what is? But the world does not frame it that way. And because it doesn't, the shopkeeper's struggles remain invisible while the entrepreneur's efforts are celebrated. For me, this gap between perception and reality has never changed what I call myself. I never felt the need to wrap my identity in fashionable language. *Dukaandaar* has been enough for me, because I know what it contains. It contains risk, resilience, accountability, and ambition. The irony may be that others hear less when I say it, but I have always heard more in it.

The Systems That Matter

One of the most important lessons I've carried with me is the power of systems. When I began, like many entrepreneurs, I did everything myself: sales, vendor negotiations, accounting, customer complaints, and even sweeping the shop floor when needed. At that time, I thought hard work alone could scale a business. But as we grew, I realized that it wasn't just effort or even the product that determined success. It was the processes and systems running behind the scenes.

I've seen this mistake play out again and again in startups. They run fast, fueled by energy and vision, chasing growth at all costs. They build flashy fronts and scale their customer numbers, but they ignore building the systems that quietly hold a company together. And then, when scale truly hits, cracks appear. It is never the product that kills you; it is the lack of systems. A strong product without strong processes is like a car without a chassis; at some point, the whole structure collapses under its own weight.

I believe every company goes through life cycles, and each stage demands a different way of thinking. First, you do everything yourself. I know this stage intimately; it teaches you the value of every function because you are the one filling every role. Then comes the second stage, when you hire all-rounders, people who are willing to jump across tasks just as you once did. They don't have titles as much as responsibilities, and they thrive in uncertainty.

The third stage is when departments begin to form. You can no longer depend on all-rounders; you need accounting handled by someone who lives and breathes numbers, operations run by someone who understands the rhythms of supply and demand, and marketing managed by people who know how to tell your story. Finally, the fourth stage is when you bring in specialists smarter than you, people whose expertise far exceeds yours in their domain. This is the stage that humbles entrepreneurs, because it requires us to step back and accept that growth now depends on others who can do things better than we ever could.

But here's the catch: if you don't prepare for these transitions with proper processes, scaling will collapse you. I learned this the hard way. In my early years, speed overshadowed structure. I thought back-end processes could wait while we focused on front-end wins. But the truth is, back-end inefficiencies are like sweet poison; they don't reveal themselves immediately, but slowly erode the foundation until one day you are staring at a crisis you can't fix overnight.

That is why I say: from day one, build systems as if you won't be there tomorrow. Your replacement should always be your first priority.

Imagine someone stepping into your role today. Could they run the company with the processes you've left behind? If the answer is no, then you haven't built a business; you've built a dependency. True entrepreneurship is not about making yourself indispensable; it's about making the company run without you. That's the discipline of systems.

Risk, Scale, and Substance

Every founder takes risks. I had mine too, except my journey didn't start from zero; it started from less than zero. I was carrying the weight of earlier failures, personal doubts, and the judgments that came with being labeled just a *dukaandaar*. That was my risk: not just financial, but emotional and reputational. I had to prove that I could build something bigger than the shop floor I stood on. But one thing I've never done is underestimate others' risks. Every entrepreneur, whether starting in a garage, a rented office, or a family shop, places their bets against uncertainty. And that gamble is never small.

What troubles me, however, is the way society glamorizes scale and style while ignoring substance. We admire companies that grow fast, raise capital, and make headlines. We celebrate valuations more than value creation. But I've learned that scaling fast is the easiest part. With enough capital and enough noise, you can inflate growth figures. The real test is whether the company has the backbone to survive once the spotlight moves elsewhere.

That backbone is built quietly, in processes, policies, and backend systems. And let me tell you, this is unglamorous work. No investor will clap for the founder who spends months refining accounting practices. No magazine cover will feature someone who stayed up nights writing down standard operating procedures. Yet these invisible efforts are what allow companies to survive storms.

I've seen it happen with peers and competitors. Companies don't collapse overnight. They don't implode in one big mistake. They erode slowly, eaten away by the weaknesses in their backend. A ledger ignored today becomes a financial hole tomorrow. A loose process in one department becomes chaos across the organization. By the time you realize the backend is failing, it's often too late to fix.

Accounting, backend systems, and processes are not glamorous, but they are essential to survival. Accounting, especially, is underestimated. People think it's clerical work anyone can do. I learned otherwise. Accounting is not just numbers on a sheet; it's a story of your company's health. If you neglect it, you are driving blind.

The backend is even trickier. It's like sweet poison. When ignored, it doesn't sting immediately. It allows you to scale, gives you the illusion of strength, and tempts you to focus only on the front end, sales, marketing, and branding. But underneath, issues compound. One day, you wake up, and the backend that was ignored has consumed the company whole. Suddenly, you're at zero. And people on the outside will say, "This happened overnight." But as someone who's lived it, I can tell you, collapse is always gradual.

That's why I keep repeating this mantra: scale is easy, sustainability is hard. True entrepreneurship is not about chasing valuation, but about building value. It's not about how fast you can scale, but how long you can last. The companies that endure are the ones that respect the backend as much as the front end.

Facing Dismissal and Doubt

Of course, I have faced my share of dismissal. I still remember emails from early hires who left, telling me I would never build anything big because I was just a shopkeeper. They told me their time was wasted. They underestimated me, and they said so in writing.

But those moments fuel me. I write down every negative comment. When someone tells me I can't do something, it ignites me. Even in college, when a professor once told me not to pursue business because I "wouldn't succeed," I carried those words with me. Years later, when I returned as a guest lecturer in marketing, I reminded him of what he had said. I said it lightly, playfully, but it meant a lot to me.

Proving people wrong is not about ego. It's about finding energy in a challenge.

Ironically, the same world that once dismissed me now calls me to mentor. Startup founders admire my ability to manage cash, vendors, and margins, things I learned only by being a dukaandaar.

Even my own brother, when he started his venture, came to me for help with finances and management. He was great at digital marketing, but the grounding of running a business, that art, came from shopkeeping.

Customers, too, have taught me lessons about the strength of local business. I remember in the early days, B2B customers like Rod and Sierra Motors, Mr. Varun and Mr. Pavan, supported me immensely. They showed me what customers value most: never saying no.

If you don't have a product today, arrange to have one by tomorrow. That's the unwritten rule of local business. Flexibility, reliability, and relationship, these are our superpowers. That's what makes a shopkeeper more than just a seller. He is a problem-solver.

Whenever a young person hesitates to take over a family business, my advice is simple: *do it.* You will save years of time, relationships, and groundwork. Even if you want to do things your own way, the foundation matters.

A family business is not a prison; it is a launchpad. Even if it gives you a one percent advantage, take it. It will save you countless struggles.

If there is one myth I want to break forever, it is that being a dukaandaar is "easy" or "unambitious." That is false. It is never easy. It takes everything from you: time, effort, patience, and resilience.

Being a shopkeeper is not a fallback. It is entrepreneurship at its most grounded, its most human.

Value Creation Over Valuation

In 2022, I had a turning point. That year, I realized real business is not about valuation, it is about value.

One incident stays with me. A middle-aged woman needed a part for her car urgently. If I had delayed by a few days, I could have made a better profit. If I delivered immediately, there was no profit, but her problem would be solved.

I chose to solve her problem. Later, she messaged me to say that my help had been critical for her family that day. That message changed me. I realized business is about being indispensable, about creating value, not chasing valuation.

So why does society glorify startups and look down on traditional businesses? I believe it's the mindset. Startups are built on hustle from day one. Family businesses, on the other hand, are weighed down by tradition, by set practices, by inherited ways of doing things.

It is far harder to change a legacy system than to build from scratch. Yet, the world often fails to see that.

But I have come to embrace it. Because while others glorify labels, I know where the real resilience lies. It lies behind the counter, in the persistence of shopkeepers who stay, who build, who endure.

Key Takeaways

- I lived through the irony of doing the same work but being seen differently depending on whether I said "shopkeeper" or "entrepreneur."

- Running a shop demanded great skills, managing cash flow, handling vendors, and solving customer issues, skills no one outside truly understood.

- I learned that society's judgment comes from its own misconceptions, not from the reality of the work.

- My time behind the counter gave me lessons no MBA could ever replicate.

- I realized that dukaandaari isn't a fallback; it is entrepreneurship in its rawest, most grounded form.

CHAPTER 3

When Change Knocks, Quick Commerce, Fast Panic

"*T*HE FIRST TIME *I saw a 10-minute delivery ad, I didn't smile. I panicked. Was my shop now 'too slow' for the modern world?"*

For years, my world revolved around predictable rhythms, the sound of shutters opening at dawn, the buzz of vendors arriving with parts, and the exchange of small talk with mechanics and loyal customers who trusted me without a second thought. Then, suddenly, a notification appeared on my phone: *"Get anything delivered in 10 minutes."*

It wasn't directed at me, not even at my line of business. But it hit me like an electric jolt. If this was what customers were beginning to expect from their morning groceries, what would they expect from us next?

That one ad was less about delivery time and more about the speed of change. And I knew, deep inside, that change had just knocked on my door, not politely, but with the force of disruption.

Quick commerce didn't directly affect the automotive accessories segment in its early days. Our world wasn't as fast-moving as the grocery or FMCG sectors. But psychologically, it changed everything. It reset the customer's mindset. People were no longer buying products; they were buying time.

It made me question everything I'd taken for granted: the pace of service, the human touch, the reliability of face-to-face business. Suddenly, every customer interaction felt like a race, not against my competitors, but against a ticking clock.

For the first time, I realized speed wasn't just a metric; it was a mindset. Quick commerce blurred the line between industries. Whether you sold spare parts or sandwiches, your customers had been reconditioned to expect immediacy. It forced me to think: how can we bring speed into an industry built on precision, relationships, and legacy? That thought became both my fear and my fuel.

The First Shockwaves

The earliest tremors weren't visible in sales; they were emotional. My customers didn't start abandoning us for apps, but they did start thinking like app users. Questions became sharper:

"Why don't you deliver?"

"Can't I just see everything online?"

"Do you have a website?"

In the automotive aftermarket, business had always been based on trust. You didn't just sell a part, you sold reliability, advice, and reassurance. But now, even in our niche, people have begun to expect seamlessness and speed. They wanted things "at one click," and it didn't matter whether we were a 300-square-foot shop or a national chain.

That was the moment I knew: technology had stopped being an advantage. It had become survival.

Panic Turns to Purpose

I remember sitting in my office one evening, staring at our ledger. It wasn't that our numbers were falling; they were steady, but the energy had shifted.

There was a silent question hanging in the air: "Are we getting left behind?"

The world outside was accelerating. Companies like Zepto, Blinkit, GoMechanic, and Spinny were scaling at unimaginable speeds. Some of them had started smaller than us but had suddenly become billion-dollar entities. It bruised my ego. We had been the veterans in our space, and yet we were moving at what felt like minus-zero speed compared to their hundredfold momentum.

That sting, that moment of bruised pride, was my turning point. I realized we weren't losing to technology; we were losing to mindset.

We were still thinking like shopkeepers while the world was moving like startups. It wasn't about apps or investors; it was about agility, adaptability, and mindset. And that realization forced me to look inward.

Traditional businesses, like ours, thrive on human relationships, but they also depend too heavily on humans. Every process, every sale, every decision was people-dependent. If a key employee fell sick, the system broke. If I weren't around, the entire shop would slow down.

It struck me one day, painfully, that I had become the bottleneck.

When I was present, everything worked perfectly. When I wasn't, nothing moved. That's when it hit me: I wasn't just the owner; I was the company's biggest liability.

So, I made a decision that terrified me. I began to remove myself from the center of operations. I started building systems that could function without me.

At first, it felt like I was erasing myself. But slowly, I began to see it differently. I wasn't removing myself; I was replacing myself with something better.

That "something better" was technology.

Everyone talks about the front end of business: websites, ads, and apps. But the real revolution happens behind the scenes.

In 2021, I made my first big leap. We began digitizing our stock system, an unglamorous but transformative move. Until then, stock-checking was a daily ritual of counting and guessing. One misplaced invoice could throw the entire day off track. But once we uploaded our entire inventory into a system, something magical happened: visibility.

Suddenly, I could check inventory, orders, and accounts from anywhere, even at home. It was liberating. It also made my father, my business partner, sit up and take notice.

He had always been quick to sense market winds, and to his credit, he didn't resist this change. We both understood that technology wasn't replacing us; it was extending us.

It allowed us to serve customers faster, reduce manual errors, and open up new channels, especially for wholesale buyers who wanted quick responses. It was a small step for the world, but a giant leap for our shop.

Of course, not everyone shared my enthusiasm. Employees wondered why I was obsessed with "this tech thing." Fellow shopkeepers whispered that I was wasting time. My income dipped for a while because I'd shifted focus from daily sales to process building.

There were nights I lay awake questioning my own decisions. Was I overthinking it? Was I drifting away from what I knew best?

Even my father and I had heated arguments. He'd ask, *"Why are we spending on software when our shelves are already full?"*

But I knew the answer, because those shelves wouldn't matter if the systems behind them collapsed.

That phase, 2021 to 2023, was brutal. Revenues dropped. Profits thinned. Transparency increased, and not everyone liked it. Systems made things visible, and visibility makes people uncomfortable. But that transparency was necessary.

In those moments, I reminded myself of something simple: short-term pain for long-term gain.

The Power of Systemization

As our operations evolved, so did our perspective. I started treating every recurring action as a process to be documented.

From how we opened the shutters, to how we greeted customers, to how payments were recorded, everything was written down. It sounds extreme, but it worked.

Within months, we had built a 40-page operations manual, our own mini "corporate handbook" for the shop. For a place that once relied entirely on muscle memory and instinct, this was a revolution.

I trained my staff not by scolding them for mistakes, but by letting them make those mistakes, and then showing them how to correct them. The goal wasn't perfection; it was independence.

I realized that leadership isn't about doing everything yourself; it's about building people who can do it better than you.

That's when I began to see a pattern: every small act of documentation was an act of scaling.

Learning to Let Go

The hardest part of the transformation wasn't implementing technology; it was changing my identity.

For years, I had been the face of the business. Customers came because they trusted me. Every major deal went through me. Every discount required my approval.

Letting go of that control was painful. I had to teach customers to trust my team, not just me. Many didn't take it well. They'd say, *"We'll come only if you're there."* And when they didn't see me, they'd walk away.

Those moments hurt more than any financial loss. I felt invisible in my own shop. But deep down, I knew that unless I made this shift, I'd never build something larger than myself.

I wasn't running a business; I was babysitting one.

So, I began pushing myself further into the background, focusing on systems, hiring specialists instead of generalists, and finding people who could own specific roles.

That shift changed everything. It gave me the freedom to think instead of react.

Breaking and Rebuilding

There were times when the stress nearly broke me. At least four times, I seriously considered shutting down the business.

Each time, something had gone wrong: customers leaving, systems failing, sales dropping. Once, when several of our major clients in the second-hand car space suddenly shut down, our revenues crashed to zero overnight.

I remember staring at the empty ledger, wondering if we had made a huge mistake by changing too much, too soon. But every time I reached the edge of giving up, something pulled me back. Sometimes it was logic, sometimes it was faith.

The biggest turning point came from something deeply personal. My mother, who had never been formally part of the company, had always been my lucky charm. During one particularly rough phase, I added her name as a shareholder, even if it was just a symbolic 0.0001%. Within a month, things turned around. Orders picked up, morale lifted, and the tide shifted.

I can't explain it logically, but that moment reminded me that some traditions are worth keeping. Not all power comes from data. Some comes from belief.

When Ego Meets Evolution

Looking back, I can see how ego disguised itself as expertise. For a long time, I believed no one could do my job as well as I could. That illusion kept me trapped.

When I started hiring specialized talent, people for accounting, tech, and customer service, it felt strange at first. But then I saw the magic of letting experts be experts.

We moved from a generalist culture to a specialist structure. Processes replaced verbal promises. Decisions became data-backed, not emotion-driven.

For the first time, the company started functioning like a company. Not a family shop, not a one-man show — but an organized, scalable entity.

The day we officially registered as a private limited company in 2021, something shifted forever. My father joked, *"From Malik, you've made me naukar."* And he was right; we were no longer owners. We were employees of a company that now stood above us.

It was humbling, but liberating. Because only when you stop owning everything can you start building something that outlasts you.

Even as we adapted, the market kept evolving faster than ever. New players, new tools, AI-driven systems — every week felt like a new disruption.

But somewhere along the journey, my fear began to fade. I started seeing technology not as a threat, but as an equalizer.

In the age of AI, a one-crore company and a thousand-crore company stand on surprisingly similar ground. Technology has flattened the playing field. What used to require massive teams and endless capital can now be done by a small, agile business with the right tools.

That's when I realized, this isn't a race against others anymore. It's a race against your own resistance.

Staying relevant doesn't mean copying every trend. It means listening closely to your customers, their pain points, their frustrations, and their expectations.

One of my oldest customers, Sierra Motors, taught me this lesson better than any business guru could. He'd buy from us not just because of our prices, but because of how we talked. We'd spend an extra two minutes listening to him, and those two minutes built more loyalty than any discount ever could.

Relevance, I realized, comes from staying human while adapting systems.

You can automate your processes, but never your relationships.

Even today, I encourage every entrepreneur I meet to ask their customers, not what they want, but what they value. Because when you know that, you'll always stay in tune with the market.

If I had to summarize the last few years in one sentence, it would be this: You don't need to change your soul, just your systems.

The heart of business hasn't changed. It's still about trust, relationships, and reliability. But the tools have changed, and so must we.

Systems are not the enemy of passion; they are the protectors of it. They give structure to creativity, control to chaos, and continuity to dreams.

Today, I no longer run a "shop." I run a company that runs without me. That's not detachment, that's evolution.

The Lesson of the Knock

When change knocked in the form of quick commerce, I panicked. But now, I see that knock differently. It wasn't a threat; it was an invitation to grow, to systemize, to evolve.

Disruption is never polite. It arrives unannounced, unsettles your comfort, and forces you to rebuild. But once you stop fighting it, it becomes your greatest teacher.

Quick commerce didn't kill traditional business; it exposed its blind spots. It reminded us that speed, data, and scalability aren't enemies of tradition. They're its modern extensions.

If there's one message I'd give to every business owner reading this, it's this: disruption doesn't destroy you, denial does.

When the next wave of change comes, don't panic. Listen. Adapt. Reimagine. Because sometimes, panic is just the first sign that evolution has begun.

Key Takeaways

- The first time I saw a 10-minute delivery, I panicked, not because it affected my industry directly, but because it changed customer expectations forever.

- That moment forced me to question systems, speed, and the pace at which my own business was evolving.

- Quick commerce taught me that customer mindsets evolve faster than industries do.

- Disruption became my teacher, not my threat.

- I realized that change doesn't destroy businesses; resisting it does.

CHAPTER 4

Corporate Lessons on the Shop Floor

THE REALIZATION DIDN'T ARRIVE in a boardroom or during a seminar. It hit me on a family holiday. I remember sitting in a resort café, trying to enjoy a cup of tea while my phone wouldn't stop buzzing. Calls from employees, messages from vendors, and unread complaints from customers. In just three days away from the shop, everything had fallen apart, orders were delayed, inventory was mismanaged, and the staff was confused about priorities. What was supposed to be a short break turned into a long week of firefighting from afar. When I returned, I found chaos, misplaced orders, missed sales, and a team that looked equally frustrated and helpless. That's when it struck me: I wasn't running a business. I was in the business. Nothing moved without me. I wasn't an entrepreneur; I was a daily-wage worker in disguise.

That was a hard pill to swallow.

For years, I had believed that being present and hustling every day was a sign of leadership. But the truth was harsher; it was a sign of dependency. The business depended on me for every small decision, every approval, and every crisis. If I weren't around, things stalled. If I took a break, it would collapse.

That's not entrepreneurship. That's entrapment.

And in that moment, I realized something crucial: if a business cannot run without you, it can never grow beyond you.

When Absence Becomes a Mirror

A couple of years later, life forced me to confront this lesson more brutally. I met with an accident in 2020 that left me bedridden for a month. I thought the systems I had begun building would hold things together. They didn't.

The daily revenue that once touched five to six lakh rupees dropped to zero within days. My phone would ring endlessly, staff unsure what to do, customers complaining, vendors waiting for direction. I felt helpless, frustrated, and even embarrassed. I had worked so hard to build a business that couldn't function without me.

That accident was not just a personal setback; it was a business wake-up call. If a single person's absence could bring an entire system to a halt, then maybe there was no system at all. I knew that the only way forward was to build something that could run, and run well, even when I wasn't there.

The First Step: From Verbal to Visible

The first and hardest step was simple to define but difficult to implement, moving from verbal to written systems.

In traditional shops, everything runs on memory, instinct, and verbal instructions. *"Bhaiya, wo order pack kar do,"* (Brother, pack that order) *"Check kar lo stock aa gaya ya nahi,"* (Check if the stock has arrived or not) *"Customer ko call kar dena."* (Call the customer). It's fast, flexible, and familiar, but dangerously fragile. When everyone assumes someone else is taking care of something, no one actually is.

I began documenting everything I did. Opening the shop, handling customer queries, updating sales, ordering inventory, closing the books, every small step. At first, it felt ridiculous. Writing down how to greet a customer, how to handle a return, and how to check availability. But when I looked more closely, I realized I had been making hundreds of micro-decisions daily that no one else even noticed.

Those invisible routines were the heartbeat of the business, and no one could hear it except me.

So, I began creating Standard Operating Procedures (SOPs) for each function. Simple, clear, and written in plain language. Every process had a flow: open, execute, report, and close. Gradually, my business started to look less like a family-run shop and more like a structured organization.

But that transition came at a price.

Resistance on the Shop Floor

When I introduced systems, the team revolted.

The people who once seemed indispensable suddenly became resistant and even hostile. They mocked the idea of writing reports or logging daily tasks. They said I was overcomplicating a "simple business." Some accused me of trying to "corporatize" our culture. Others quietly stopped cooperating.

In the beginning, we were a team of 25. Within months of system implementation, 23 left. It was one of the toughest phases of my life. I had believed that structure would unite the team; instead, it scattered them. But as painful as it was, that exodus revealed something I had never seen clearly: who was genuinely aligned with the company's growth, and who was merely comfortable in the chaos.

Two people stayed. Just two.

They weren't the most experienced, but they believed in the vision. Together, we rebuilt from scratch, using systems as the foundation, not people's moods or availability. That's when I learned a leadership truth I still hold close: systems don't replace people; they reveal them.

The Systems Revolution

The next phase was all about translating structure into action. I wanted my shop to function like a miniature corporation, not in spiritless bureaucracy, but in clarity and accountability.

We introduced an ERP (Enterprise Resource Planning) system. Earlier, billing was the only recorded activity. Everything else, procurement, delivery, follow-ups, vendor payments, happened in silos. With the ERP, every process became visible. Tasks were mapped. Responsibilities were logged. Accountability was no longer verbal; it was data-driven.

The difference was immediate. We could now see who was doing what, when, and how well. If a customer complaint arose, we could trace it back to the exact point of failure, whether it was procurement, packing, or delivery. Suddenly, decisions were no longer based on assumptions but on evidence.

Our productivity increased exponentially, almost a hundredfold in the first few months. But it wasn't just about faster numbers. It was about clarity. For the first time, I wasn't operating in the dark.

We also implemented task automation apps to delegate and monitor daily activities. Every task, from inventory checks to customer calls, was logged. Employees knew what was expected, when it was due, and how it would be evaluated. The transparency was uncomfortable at first, but it gradually built a new culture of accountability.

And then something magical happened: growth became predictable.

The Clash of Old and New

With every new system came a new challenge, skepticism.

Some customers complained that our processes made things "slow." Some employees grumbled that *we were becoming too corporate.*

Even family members raised eyebrows. They said, *"Why complicate a simple shop with all this data and software?"*

At first, their words stung. I questioned myself. Maybe I was overengineering things. But over time, the results silenced the doubts. We began to see consistent growth, fewer errors, happier customers, and more time to think strategically.

My father, too, was skeptical initially. But as he saw the system work, he became my biggest supporter. His experience balanced my data-driven approach. He would often remind me, *"Numbers can tell you what's happening, but not always why."* And he was right.

That's when I understood, discipline and data don't replace intuition and experience. They enhance it.

The sweet spot lies in the marriage of both; intuition tells you where to look, and data tells you what's true.

Professionalization Does Not Mean Corporatization

One of the biggest misconceptions about systemization is that it makes your business impersonal. People think discipline means detachment, that if you put processes in place, you'll lose the human touch.

I couldn't disagree more.

Systems don't make a business robotic; they make it sustainable. In fact, they protect the human side by removing chaos. When your team isn't firefighting daily, they can focus on serving customers better, building relationships, and innovating.

We used to joke that our ERP became our "silent co-founder." It didn't complain, it didn't forget, and it didn't take days off. It simply worked, consistently, accurately, and without emotion. That's what allowed me to step back and think like a leader instead of an operator.

Today, I often tell fellow shop owners that your replacement isn't another person. It's a system. Humans will always fall short when you compare them to your own standards. But systems, when designed well, don't compete with you; they complete you.

When the Numbers Tell the Truth

One of the most humbling moments came when I compared our financials before and after systemization.

For years, we had believed we were earning well. But when we began tracking actual data, we realized a painful truth: we were burning more than we were earning. There were leakages, inefficiencies, unbilled work, and unnecessary wastage that had gone unnoticed because we were relying on gut feel. When the data came in, it was clear that our "success" was inflated by chaos. It was the first time I truly understood the phrase, you can't grow what you don't track.

Numbers don't lie, but they do reveal. They reveal inefficiency, complacency, and sometimes even self-deception. The shift from intuition to information was uncomfortable but liberating. I could finally make decisions based on facts rather than feelings.

Even today, I rely on about 65% on data and 35% on instinct. Ideally, that ratio should tilt more towards data because instinct, while invaluable, is subjective. Data brings objectivity. Together, they create balance, one rooted in wisdom, the other in truth.

Of course, this transformation wasn't smooth. We faced multiple failures, some frustrating, others enlightening.

One of the biggest was the interlinking of branches and departments. In our early system design, we treated each unit as independent. That created gaps, communication leaks, duplication of work, and accountability blind spots. It took months to identify and fix those structural holes.

Another was the adoption of automation tools. I once spent six months just convincing people to use a simple task management app. It felt like dragging a mountain uphill. The resistance was psychological; people feared being tracked, judged, or replaced. But persistence paid off. Once they saw the benefit, reduced confusion, and clear accountability, they couldn't imagine working without it.

The lesson was clear: every new system faces resistance, not because it's wrong, but because it demands responsibility. As the systems matured, I learned another profound truth: Delegation **is leadership**.

Before, I used to do everything myself. I believed it was faster, safer, and more accurate. But in reality, it was suffocating the company's growth. Every time I held on to a task, I was holding back someone else's opportunity to grow, and the company's chance to scale.

I began mapping my daily activities, from small operational decisions to major strategic ones. Then, one by one, I asked myself, *"Can this be delegated or systemized?"* If the answer was yes, it moved off my plate. If not, I built a process around it so that it could be handled without me next time.

That single exercise changed everything.

The more I delegated, the freer I became to focus on vision and strategy. And surprisingly, the business didn't fall apart; it flourished. Because delegation isn't about giving away power; it's about multiplying it. Today, I tell every founder I meet that if you can't delegate, you're not leading; you're merely managing. A one-man army may win a battle, but never a war.

The real test of leadership isn't how well your business performs when you're present, it's how well it performs when you're absent.

I used to be the engine. Now, I've become the architect. I no longer run the machine; I design how it runs. That's the transformation every business owner must aim for.

When you build systems, you create freedom for yourself and for your team. You create predictability in performance, accountability in execution, and scalability in growth. The chaos turns into clarity. The dependency turns into discipline. And the business begins to breathe on its own.

That's the moment you stop being just a shopkeeper and start becoming a true entrepreneur.

Key Takeaways

- When a short holiday led to chaos in the shop, I finally saw how dependent everything was on me.

- I wasn't running a business; I was trapped inside it.

- That experience forced me to accept that true growth requires systems, not heroic effort.

- Delegation and process-building became the only way to free myself from daily firefighting.

- I understood that a real business must run without me, not because I am irrelevant, but because the systems are strong

Fathers and Founders The Generational Tug of War

I N BUSINESS MEETINGS, I spoke with logic. At home, I spoke with hesitation. After all, how do you pitch a new idea to the man who taught you everything?

People often assume that a father and son working together must have always shared a deep, seamless bond. In my case, the bond came much later. Before I entered the business, my relationship with my father was simple and limited. We crossed paths like two people living under the same roof but in different time zones. He returned home late, long after I had gone to sleep, because school awaited me the next morning. I left early, long before he woke up. Most of our conversations happened through my mother or around routine matters. There were no long discussions, no shared hobbies, and definitely no common ground.

Our relationship looked like any ordinary father and son dynamic. We argued about small things. We went through days of silence because there was no topic to connect us. When I left to pursue my MBA, the gap widened. I spoke to my mother more than to my father, and the only conversations we had were transactional and work-related whenever I visited the shop. I sometimes wondered if we would ever build the kind of connection that people talk about in stories.

Ironically, business created the bond that life could not. When I joined the business, when we finally had a common mission, we found the missing bridge. Conversations that earlier felt forced now came naturally. Business became the thread that tied us together. Today, I talk more to my father than to my mother, not because of preference, but because we share a domain where we both feel at home.

Looking back, I understand something important. Sometimes a relationship does not grow through shared emotions. Sometimes it grows through shared responsibilities.

Two Chairs, Two Roles

When people ask me how I manage the dual roles of being a son at home and a professional in the office, I tell them that it begins with a decision. I once made a simple rule for myself: at the office, he is the chairman; at home, he is my father. These worlds should not collide. At work, our conversations are structured, documented, and taken seriously. At home, they are open, light, and often inconclusive because home is not governed by process.

From the day we incorporated our private limited company, we followed a clear method. Every meeting was recorded. Every discussion was documented. Even when it was just the two of us, we made minutes of meetings and circulated them officially. This was not to complicate our relationship. It was to protect it. Once everything was on paper, decisions were no longer personal victories or defeats. They became organizational outcomes.

People romanticize the idea of a family business. They picture warm discussions over tea, quick decisions during dinner, and an easy blending of personal and professional life. The truth is very different. Boundaries are essential. Without them, business can damage the home, and home can paralyze the business.

The clarity that saved our relationship came from separation. In the office, I accepted that he was the leader I had to learn from. At home, he accepted that I was his son who did not need to perform.

Earning My Place at the Table

I have heard countless stories of second-generation entrepreneurs who had to fight for their voice. Surprisingly, I did not face that resistance. My father is a very practical man. When I entered the business, he did not restrict me. He gave me space, freedom, and responsibilities from day one. He treated me like someone who had to prove himself through work, not through his surname.

When people ask me how I earned my voice, I tell them that I did not earn it through a designation. I earned it through accountability. I did not call myself MD or CEO. I did not even have an ID card. I saw myself as a representative of Car Trends, nothing more. My voice mattered because I carried weight in the work I did.

We decided early on which departments each of us would focus on. If a decision involved both areas and we disagreed, the department head became the deciding authority. If even then the conflict remained unresolved, the final accountability came to me. This was an unsaid agreement, but a powerful one. It kept our hierarchy clear yet flexible.

I realize now that the reason I found acceptance was that the environment was intentionally designed that way. We both respected the same principle. A designation does not give you a voice. Ownership of responsibility does.

The First Major Disagreement

Every father-son partnership looks smooth until the first major disagreement appears. For us, it came early. When we had the shop, I believed that to scale, we needed to shift from front-end operations to back-end infrastructure and expansion. My father disagreed. For him, being at the front desk had always been the heart of the business. Meeting customers, building relationships, handling sales, and negotiating were his strengths.

The idea that I wanted to move away from the shop floor and build the backend operations looked risky and unnecessary to him. People questioned the decision. They told him it was a mistake. They told him I was making the wrong move. I still remember what he told me. He said, *"If you believe this will work, do it. But be ready to handle the consequences."*

This disagreement became the start of something bigger. It taught both of us that our difference in thinking was not a threat. It was a necessity. He brought experience. I brought perspective. Together, we brought direction.

The Challenge of Change

Change is uncomfortable for everyone, but it is particularly complex in a family business. My father is practical, disciplined, and sharp, but operationally, he came from a world where relationships mattered more than processes. He spoke to everyone directly. Whether it was a salesperson, a technician, or an accountant, his involvement was direct and personal.

When we introduced the ERP system, it became one of the biggest shifts in the company. Suddenly, processes took precedence over personal interactions. Data replaced verbal updates. Structured departments replaced open access. At first, it was difficult for him. But one thing I admire about my father is that he never resisted anything that helped the company.

He questioned the change, yes. But he questioned it to align himself with it, not to oppose it.

The operational gap between us was clear. He valued relationships and instinct. I valued systems and structure. Yet digitally, we were surprisingly aligned. He is actually very data-driven. Once he understood the purpose, he supported every technological change we implemented.

In many ways, his openness became the foundation of our transformation. But that did not mean everything was easy.

Protection or Resistance

People often assume that fathers in business are protective. In my case, my father never showed overt protection. He told me something very powerful early on. He said, "You are your own backup." That statement changed everything. It made me responsible for my decisions. It also made me fearless.

My mother, on the other hand, was always anxious. Mothers naturally worry when their children take risks. She did not want me to face failure, conflict, or pressure. But my father allowed me to fight my battles. He gave me the freedom to fail and the space to learn.

His support was silent but strong. He never stopped me. He never discouraged me. Even when I made decisions that were unconventional or unpopular in the industry, he did not interfere. That freedom built my confidence.

Ironically, I sometimes felt more protective of him than he ever felt of me.

Cultural Values and Emotional Loyalties

Working with an elder in business, particularly a father, means navigating cultural expectations. In India, the idea that "elders know best" carries emotional weight. Experience matters. Relationships matter. Loyalty matters.

My father built deep relationships with vendors and customers. Because of those connections, I had access to opportunities that others in my industry could only dream of. Vendors respected him. Customers trusted him. His relationships were not transactional. They were personal. That legacy helped me enormously.

But emotional loyalty also created complications. Some old relationships limited our progress. There were instances when we were taken for granted. There were times when the relationship became more important than the system. I used to disagree. I believed that business should not be dictated by personal emotion. It should serve the company.

This clash became one of our recurring battles. He looked at relationships as assets. I looked at them as variables. Over time, we learned to balance both. His relationships built the brand. My systems protected it.

The Days I Wanted to Quit

People assume that second-generation entrepreneurs have it easy. They inherit a running business and a stable foundation. The truth is often the opposite. When you are trying to modernize something built traditionally, you fight a silent, ongoing battle.

There were many days when I felt like giving up. Sometimes I would ask myself why I was fighting so hard for change that no one else seemed to want. I am often seen as the one who argues, pushes, and fights. And on some days, the weight of that reputation felt unbearable.

Why was I putting myself through this? Why could I not live a normal, comfortable life? Why did every step of progress feel like a battle?

The answer always came back to the same truth. If I stopped pushing today, the business's future would remain dependent on chance rather than structure. If I wanted this company to become something stronger than any individual, I had to go through the discomfort. Progress is painful when you are the first one walking that path.

Surprising Results and Unexpected Validation

Among the many decisions we took, one of the most surprising outcomes came from the inventory management overhaul. For years, we handled inventory ourselves. It felt natural since we had grown up managing it. But as business expanded, inefficiencies increased. Data became unreliable. Shrinkage became unpredictable. Processes were inconsistent.

Outsourcing inventory management to professionals was a bold move. My father did not like it initially. To him, it felt like losing control of something sacred. But once the system came into place, he saw the results clearly. For years, we prided ourselves on our inventory experience. Suddenly, professionals showed us gaps we had never noticed.

This success gave him confidence in my decisions. It showed him that my intention was not to replace his experience but to strengthen the company.

Aligning Decision Making

Our decision-making styles are different. He relies on instinct backed by decades of experience. I rely on data supported by systems. To manage these differences, we created a rule. We define a process or workflow, freeze it for at least three months, and follow it strictly. If a situation falls outside the defined process, we discuss it before acting.

This rule created clarity. It reduced emotional reactions. It minimized misunderstandings. Most importantly, it gave both of us a framework to lean on. Instead of arguing based on personal beliefs, we evaluated based on documented processes.

It was not a perfect system, but it helped us respect each other's approach.

One of the biggest compromises I made was understanding that the company is bigger than both of us. My personal opinions are irrelevant if they do not align with company policy. This principle helped build trust across the entire organization.

Earlier, employees saw me as a young boy they could approach directly. Their issues depended on my mood. Whether it was solved or delayed felt personal. Over time, I learned that this was unhealthy. Today, every process is system-driven. People interact with the company, not with my mood.

A compromise that shaped me deeply was the one I never expressed. I learned to listen. I learned to observe silently before responding. I learned to accept feedback from anyone, even someone younger or more junior. Silent compromises do not weaken authority. They strengthen maturity.

There was no single moment when my father began trusting my judgment. It happened gradually. After we incorporated the company in 2021, revenue grew, systems stabilized, and dependency reduced. Sales continued even when we were not present. That was the turning point. Every shopkeeper knows that if business stops in your absence, you are not running a business; you are running a counter. When sales started happening without us, my father realized that the company was finally becoming bigger than any one person.

For the first time, he saw the company as a living entity and not a personal identity.

A Subtle Role Reversal

Over time, I noticed a shift. My father began asking for my perspective more often. Not in a formal way, but in subtle moments.

Whether it was about back-end structure or front-end operations, he began including my viewpoint in a natural, unforced way. He never declared that he trusted me more. But his actions showed it. Data spoke louder than pride.

His leadership evolved. Instead of telling people what to do, he started showing them results and letting the numbers speak. I witnessed a man who spent decades believing in the power of instinct now embracing the strength of systems.

This role reversal did not diminish him. It elevated both of us.

People often ask me if my father sees me as a partner or as a successor. For years, I felt like a partner. Today, I believe he sees me as a successor. Not because I demanded it, but because the company needed it. He still calls himself the co-founder of the decisions we make. That humility is rare.

My philosophy remains simple. A successful business is one that can run without its promoters. If I step away one day, the company should remain unaffected. That is the mark of a true legacy.

If I had to describe my father's leadership style in one phrase, he is a one-man army. He can survive anything, anywhere, without anyone. That survival instinct is his strength.

My leadership style is different. I believe in first doing the task myself, mastering it, and then delegating it. If I find myself doing the same task three times, I look for someone who can take it forward. I believe that repeated tasks create bottlenecks, and bottlenecks limit growth. Delegation is not about handing off work. It is about buying time for strategy.

Legacy, Sacrifice, and The Weight of Responsibility

My father sacrificed significantly for the business. He gave up personal time, entertainment, rest, and leisure. Most of his life was dedicated to providing for us. Tomorrow, if someone asks me what shaped my sense of responsibility, I will say it was the sacrifices I saw him make without ever mentioning them.

Someday, when the company goes public, I know that will be our moment of celebration. Not because it marks financial success but because it symbolizes every silent sacrifice he made and every silent fight I undertook.

If I could speak to my younger self, I would tell him this. Whatever your father built might look small, scattered, or imperfect to you, but it holds seeds of possibility. Use them. Enhance them. Build on them. You do not start from zero. You start from the pieces he has gathered over a lifetime. Growth is not about rejecting the past. It is about building from it.

Key Takeaways
- Working with my father taught me emotional lessons that no business book ever could.

- His trust in me didn't change overnight, it happened gradually, as results spoke louder than words

- Over time, our roles shifted naturally, and I grew from a partner into a successor.

- Our leadership styles are different, but our goals align to build something that outlives both of us.

- I realized that legacy is not about rejecting the past; it is about building on the sacrifices made before us.

Chapter 6

Branding a Legacy Business

I STILL REMEMBER THE first time it hit me that my shop needed branding. It was 2021, and I was sitting at the counter like I had done a thousand times before. Nothing dramatic was happening. No crisis. No competition chasing me. No customer complaints. Just an ordinary day. Yet something inside me shifted. I realized that if I wanted the business to grow beyond me, then it could not depend on me. The only thing that could replace me was the company itself. And for the company to stand on its own, it needed a brand.

For years, people came to the shop and said they had bought something from Prateek's shop, wanted to speak to Prateek, or would only deal with Prateek. Even when we had a growing team, customers would insist that I handle the work because they knew me in the B2B sector. It was flattering at first. Later, it became suffocating. I could see my own team feeling demotivated when customers dismissed their presence and insisted that only I could get things done. They were capable, they were hard working, but the perception outside was that everything revolved around me.

That was the moment when I realized that my business could never grow if it continued to carry only my name. I did not want people to say they were going to Prateek's shop. I wanted them to say they were going to Car Trends. I wanted people who joined the company to feel that they were joining a brand, not an individual's office. I wanted identity, structure, and collective importance. I wanted a name that would outlive me. That was the birth of our shop's branding. Not because we wanted to look modern. Not because we wanted to impress younger customers. Not because competition was rising. It was because I wanted to replace myself. It was because the business was becoming difficult to scale without systems that could stand on their own, independent of any one person. And it was because the more we grew, the more we needed technology, process design, and consistency to build something larger than my own presence.

Branding was not a marketing move. It was a survival decision.

The First Time Someone Called Us a Brand

A few months after that moment of realization, something happened that I still smile about. I was sitting at the counter when a man walked in. He did not know who I was. He did not recognize me as the owner. He had come through our website and asked, very casually, whether this was Car Trends and whether it was the same brand he had seen online.

He never asked for Prateek. He never asked for the owner or the manager. He wanted Car Trends. I cannot explain the feeling that went through me in that moment. For the first time, my personal identity stepped aside, and the brand stepped forward. I felt proud, grateful, and strangely relieved. It was the moment that confirmed we were building something beyond a shop. We were building an entity.

Giving the Shop an Identity

Once the realization set in, we began shaping the identity of the business. We started by documenting everything. We wrote down the sales process from start to finish.

We wrote down the purchase process in detail. We created SOPs. We worked on our ERP. We made sure that every customer interaction went through a single centralized number. We created a uniform communication style and built a small script so every member of our team could speak to customers in the same tone and approach.

We wrote down the feedback customers gave us. Not in an emotional way, but in a structured way so we could study it, understand it, and act on it. We set up systems that would allow anyone to be replaced by someone else if required. The idea was simple. The business should run on the strength of processes, not personalities. It should be built on systems, not individuals.

I often say this openly. We created these processes to replace me. And that is exactly how it all started.

We never hired a branding expert. For a long time, we could not afford one. Even now, we do not have a dedicated branding person in the company. Instead, we rely on our people who interact with customers daily. They know what customers think. They know the end consumer's mindset and behavior. That ground-level understanding has been far more valuable to us than any fancy branding strategy.

Our branding has been built by real people doing real work. Not slides, not theories, not consultants. Just experience, observation, and honest feedback.

The Name and the Logo

The name Car Trends came to us quite abruptly. We were thinking about trends and how the automotive world keeps evolving, and the name just clicked. It felt symbolic, modern, and future-ready. We were moving into a multi-brand arena and needed a name that could adapt to different segments of the four-wheeler market.

In college, I learned an unusual framework for branding. We were taught that every brand is like an animal, a flower, and a fruit. Which animal represents our brand energy? Which flower represents its feeling? Which fruit represents its flavor or appeal? Those questions helped me think about the kind of identity I wanted for Car Trends.

So, the logo and the name were built around that idea. Something relatable. Something that could be idolized. Something modern. Something flexible.

Understanding Branding Through Starbucks

I did not research other businesses extensively, but one brand influenced my thinking without me intending it. Starbucks.

I noticed how people feel proud when someone calls out their name for a coffee. It makes people feel seen. It creates a sense of identity and belonging. I realized that people flaunt where they go. It is strange but true. We love telling people where we bought something from. We love associating ourselves with brands because it gives us a sense of pride.

So, I imagined people saying, I went to Car Trends the same way they say I went to Starbucks or McDonald's. That small idea created a healthy FOMO and made us work toward a brand identity we could proudly speak about. In the beginning, my family did not understand branding at all. To them, a shop name was just a shop name. They felt any name would do. There was no concept of brand image, identity, or positioning. They simply wanted to know the name of the shop so customers could locate it. For them, branding felt unnecessary. For me, it was the foundation of the future.

I was always experimenting with changes. Sometimes I changed the direction of the counters. Sometimes the layout of the shop. Sometimes the table where I sat. Every time my parents visited, they would ask why things had changed again.

For me, change created motivation. For them, change created worry.

But when it came to branding, surprisingly, there was no conflict. There were discussions, maybe confusion, but never real resistance. We took time to finalize the name and logo, but no one stopped the process.

Even as we stepped into modern branding, I made it a point to retain emotional connections with old customers. I still meet them personally. I greet them, wish them, sit with them, and check on them. I even meet them during festivals or reach out once every few months just to stay connected.

In India, emotional connection is everything. Once people feel that connection, sales happen automatically. I encourage my team to do the same. The more we keep that personal bond alive, the stronger the brand becomes.

What Old Customers Taught Me About Our Brand

Customers taught me something very important. A brand is built by the customer, not by the owner. You can spend crores on branding, marketing, campaigns, or hiring high-budget teams. But unless your customers vouch for you, the brand will not last.

Customers build long-term brands. Owners only build the starting point. I often ask customers why they buy from us. Some say they buy it because it is my shop. Some say it is because they get the right product. Some say they do not know anyone else who supplies these parts. Their answers sometimes make me happy and at other times disturb me. But they always help me understand what the brand truly means to them.

Stories That Changed Everything

There are two stories that have completely shaped my view of our brand. One was when a young boy damaged his father's car. The part he needed was unavailable everywhere. He was scared to face his father.

When he came to us, we were lucky to have the part. The relief he felt was so real that he hugged us. The next day, his father came to thank us and brought us something as a gesture of appreciation. That moment made me realize that we do not just trade parts. We help people. We solve problems. We make life easier for families.

The second story was about a woman who was the sole earner in her household. She had two kids and also took care of her parents and in-laws. Her car was essential for everything. She had been struggling to find a certain part. When she found it on our web portal, it changed everything for her. That made me see Car Trends as a brand that supported people in practical, meaningful ways.

Before branding, customers used to say things like Prateek ki dukaan. After branding, people began saying Car Trends. That shift was powerful.

Even our employees felt more united because they were a part of something bigger. Suddenly, they were not just working in a shop. They were part of a brand.

There were many turning points. But the biggest one was when purchases and sales started coming in because of the brand, not because of me. Vendors and customers began trusting the company name more than the individual. That was when I realized that branding had transformed our identity.

It was no longer a one-man or two-man show. It was a brand show.

Many customers discovered us online and then became loyal offline customers. People living close to our branches would find us online, realize we were nearby, and visit the shop. Workshops would come directly to buy parts and get them fitted.

This confirmed something for me. The future belongs to businesses that exist both online and offline. Only online will not be enough.

Digital Strategy That Worked for Us

I am not a technical person, so I needed something simple. Shopify was perfect for us because we could manage it without technical expertise. Google also worked well for us because our products were niche, and photos and details were not available globally. These two platforms became our backbone.

For us, social media was never about generating leads. It was only for branding and visibility. We wanted people to know we existed.

One review on Team BHP about an engine cover led to many orders. That taught me the power of visibility and feedback.

In the early days, content creation was difficult. We did not have enough to work with. Today, it is much easier because tools and ideas are everywhere. But consistency is still the biggest factor. When you stay, you grow. Even when you feel like you are not growing, consistency pushes you ahead because others fall back.

We get many negative reviews. Our business is complicated. Every car has thousands of parts, and every model is different. Mistakes happen. Instead of deleting reviews, we try to fix the issue behind them. It is still a challenge, but we keep learning. We work hard. We try. We help. Ours is a thankless industry, but our goal is to make people feel thankful by solving their problems honestly and patiently.

If our shop could speak, it would say: We will try to solve your problem. And if we cannot, we will find a way to help you solve it.

Every day we experiment with something new. There is no perfect state. There is always a better version possible. We keep our core values intact while constantly striving to be better than the previous day.

Branding changed how I looked at my own shop. Today, I never say my shop. I say the Car Trends company. I never say my office. I say the Car Trends office. Branding shifted my mindset from ownership to stewardship.

The hardest part of branding was accepting that the company was becoming bigger than me. It was no longer about me doing everything. It was about the brand doing everything.

I want the next generation to focus on core values. To understand why they exist. To know what they want to represent. To take initiative. To create mechanisms that survive beyond individual effort.

Branding is not optional. Without a brand, your shop will survive only as long as you are there. After you are gone, it will fade. With a brand, your shop can outlive you. Without a brand, you become your own enemy, because everything depends on you.

Not yet. We have a long way to go. But we are on the path. And that is what matters.

Branding did not change who we are. It helped us express who we already were. It gave shape to a story that had always been alive but never spoken clearly. It helped us build identity, clarity, and pride. Most importantly, it helped us create a brand that could stand on its own, independent of me. A brand that could grow beyond a counter. A brand that could last.

Key takeaways

- Observing seasoned shopkeepers made me appreciate the instincts and speed they operate with, skills no classroom teaches

- never relied on fancy titles; I've always been comfortable calling myself a dukaandaar.

- I saw how the world reacts differently to "entrepreneur," even when the work is exactly the same

- My challenge became shifting the narrative: showing that shopkeeping is modern, ambitious, and deeply entrepreneurial.

- Systems, not labels, became the backbone of our brand transformation.

CHAPTER 7

The People Business Not Just Customers

GREW UP BELIEVING that customers were the heart of the business. Every business book says it. Every consultant says it. Every shopkeeper believes it. But the deeper I went into building Car Trends, the more I realized something very different. Customers matter, yes, but the people who stand behind the counter matter just as much. Sometimes even more. They shape the culture, they carry the workload, they anchor the customer's trust, and they become the invisible hands that keep the business together.

It took me years to understand that business is not only about customers. It is about people. Your team. Your vendors. Your partners. Your family. Your ecosystem. That is the real business. And the day you understand this, your entire view of growth changes.

I often say this openly. Culture is the ultimate cost shield in a business. It protects you from mistakes, misunderstandings, inefficiencies, and unnecessary wastage. Culture reduces friction. Culture increases ownership. Culture holds the business together when everything else is shaking. And I have learned all this not from textbooks, but from mistakes, conflicts, and long nights when I had no one to blame except myself.

Why Culture Became My First Real Lesson in Leadership

For me, culture began with one simple realization. I cannot do everything. I work seventeen to eighteen hours a day because that is how I am built. I have energy, passion, and a stubbornness that keeps me awake long after the shop shuts. But I never wanted employees who simply follow instructions for a salary. I wanted people who behaved like owners, who developed themselves like owners, and who felt they were building something meaningful with me.

Culture is how we behave inside and outside. How do we talk to each other? How we listen. How we handle problems. How we respond to customers in pain. Because let me tell you something very clearly. Our industry runs entirely on customer pain. Nobody buys spare parts for fun. Nobody wakes up happy about repair work. They come to us because something is broken. Our job is not to add more pain. Our job is to reduce it.

This mindset itself is cultural. It is not a process. It is not an SOP. It is an instinct.

I remember a story of a restaurant where the owner shut the entire outlet because he found one stale item. He flew in himself, tested everything, and only reopened when he was satisfied. That is culture. That is discipline. That is ownership.

I wanted something similar for Car Trends. Not grand gestures. But a value system where we take action on mistakes, not hide them. Where we solve a customer's pain, not pass it around. Where the team feels proud of the work, not just responsible for it.

The Hidden Cost of Poor Culture

People often assume money leaks only through wrong decisions or market downturns. But in my experience, the highest hidden cost comes from poor culture.

Miscommunication. No communication. Confusion. Blame games. Lack of training. Wrong assumptions. These invisible cracks destroy efficiency.

There was a time when we assumed new employees would be ready from day one. We handed over responsibilities, believing they would take ownership by default. But ownership does not come without understanding. And understanding does not come without training.

Our biggest mistake was believing that every new person would learn on the job. But every company has a different system. A different style. A different complexity. Without proper orientation, people become confused, and mistakes multiply.

Misguided processes lead to rework.

Rework leads to frustration.

Frustration leads to disengagement.

Disengagement leads to poor performance.

Poor performance leads to higher costs.

It took me a long time to accept that the problem was not the people. The problem was us. We had never built a culture of clarity. We had never documented our processes. We had never trained people properly. We had never created a system of checks, follow-ups, and accountability.

Today, everything is written down. Every process. Every rule. Every expectation. Each new employee reads, trains, and shadows before taking full charge. And it has changed the entire rhythm of the company.

When Culture Turns Toxic: A Hard Lesson

I used to believe that culture naturally grows stronger as the business grows. I imagined that, with time, experience, and maturity, our people would evolve together and that the organization would adapt automatically. I could not have been more wrong. Culture does not grow with the business. Culture gets tested with the business.

And some of the harshest lessons I have learned came from the most toxic phases.

One of the biggest shocks came when we decided to streamline our warehouse operations. Inventory management had become complex. We needed more accuracy, better checks, and a cleaner process flow. After evaluating our options, we decided to outsource the operational layer to a 3PL company. They were supposed to run the day-to-day warehouse functions while our existing warehouse staff would step back and supervise, verify, and focus on higher-level responsibilities.

On paper, it sounded perfect. We believed it would free up our old team from their routine responsibilities and allow them to focus on efficiency rather than doing the manual work themselves. We thought they would welcome the change. Instead, it created a storm.

The resistance began quietly. A comment here, a complaint there. But soon it became a daily pattern. Something was always wrong. Either the 3PL team had counted something incorrectly, placed something in the wrong bin, or failed to update a sheet on time. Every day, there was a new reason to point fingers. What frustrated me most was that, when I looked more closely, the mistakes were not necessarily due to the new 3PL team. Many times, the old issues that had existed in our earlier system were simply surfacing more clearly. But instead of acknowledging this, our team chose the easier route of blaming the newcomers.

It took me some time to understand what was actually happening. The problem was not the 3PL company. The problem was not even the mistakes. The real issue was resistance. Our people did not want someone else entering their territory. They were used to a certain way of working, and now someone from the outside was changing their rhythm. Even if the change was good, it felt threatening. And when change feels threatening, culture turns defensive.

This was when I learned the first rule of toxic culture. Toxicity does not begin with big conflicts. It begins with small fears.

Whenever something new enters an organization, friction is guaranteed. It does not matter whether it is new technology, new leadership, new process design, or new structure. Change challenges people because it exposes weaknesses. It questions comfort zones. It demands accountability. A stable culture adjusts and evolves. A fragile culture resists and reacts. And ours, at that time, was not as strong as I thought.

Another lesson came when we introduced new reporting software. For years, our reporting had been manual. It was slow, inconsistent, and often incomplete. We needed a transparent system where every order, every movement, every responsibility, and every timeline was visible to the right people. It was supposed to bring discipline, clarity, and speed.

Instead, it triggered chaos.

People said the software was confusing. They said it was slowing them down. They said it was unnecessary. They said the old way was better. Some even complained that they did not have the time to learn something new. Every excuse came out except the real reason. The truth was simple. They did not want to be accountable.

Before the software, mistakes could be hidden. After the software, mistakes became visible. Before the software, inefficiencies could be blamed on circumstances. After the software, the numbers spoke clearly. The resistance had nothing to do with technology. It had everything to do with fear. Fear of being exposed. Fear of being questioned. Fear of losing importance. Fear of becoming replaceable.

I realized something very important during this phase. Culture does not get revealed during stable times. Culture gets revealed the moment change walks in. Until then, everyone seems united. Everyone seems positive. Everyone seems cooperative.

But when you introduce something new, people's true mindset comes to the surface. You see who adapts quickly. You see who silently supports. You see who resists openly. You see who creates negativity. And you also see who pulls others down to avoid being pulled down themselves.

These experiences taught me that toxic culture is not built by bad people. It is built by insecure people. And insecurity stems from unclear communication, responsibilities, future paths, and expectations. We had never prepared our team mentally for growth. We had improved systems, but not mindsets. We had upgraded processes, but not perspectives.

Looking back, the mistakes were not theirs alone. We had not explained the purpose of the change clearly enough. We had not trained them patiently. We had not reassured them that new systems were meant to support them, not replace them. We had not involved them in the transition. Change done without communication feels like punishment. Change done with clarity feels like progress.

The toxic phase eventually passed, but it left a lasting lesson. Culture is not built through posters, meetings, or policy documents. Culture is built through conversations, clarity, and confidence. When people feel secure, they adapt faster. When they feel involved, they participate. When they feel valued, they support growth. And when they feel insecure, everything collapses.

Today, whenever we introduce something new, I do not begin with the process. I begin with the people. I explain the change. I answer questions. I repeat the purpose. I make sure everyone understands how it will help them. This does not completely remove friction, but it turns resistance into cooperation rather than toxicity.

Culture is not tested when things stay the same. Culture is tested when things change. And real culture survives the change.

How Leaders Create Culture Without Saying a Word

I believe something very strongly. Whatever the leader does becomes the rule. And whatever the leader ignores becomes acceptable behavior.

If I break one rule, my employees will break a hundred. If I delay one report, they will delay ten. If I am careless with one procedure, they will be careless with many. If I do not respect the policies I create, then no one else will take them seriously.

Leadership is not about giving instructions. Leadership is about being an example.

There was a time when we did not have a proper billing policy. Now we do. But if I myself bypass the billing policy even once, the whole effort collapses. Employees watch us more than they listen to us.

Precision thinking begins at the top. If I respond on time, they respond on time. If I handle pressure with discipline, they try to do the same. If I treat people with respect, the culture follows that tone.

Rituals That Build Discipline

People think rituals are big celebrations. For me, rituals are simple things done consistently. Following SOPs. Treating every person with dignity. Train every employee as if they will lead tomorrow. Giving responsibility, not just tasks. These small habits create discipline.

We treat everyone the same way, whether someone is a security guard or a senior executive. Everyone's work has value. Everyone deserves respect.

Our culture is built on the mindset that anyone can rise. Anyone can lead. Anyone can grow. And when people believe that, their behavior changes automatically.

Confusion is expensive. Clarity saves time, energy, and relationships. Every employee must know exactly:

What they are responsible for

How they will be evaluated

What is considered good work

What is considered poor work

Where can they improve

Where they will be questioned

Without this, you invite misunderstandings, stress, and silence.

Not everyone is meant to be an all-rounder. And that is okay. But every person must know what is expected of them. Not ten things. Just their core role. With that clarity, they take ownership.

Leadership behavior affects costs. It affects morale. It affects discipline. How a leader behaves under pressure reveals the true culture of the company.

I have seen situations where one leadership decision created a ripple effect. For example, our sales team often builds strong relationships with customers. But when policies get stricter, customers sometimes challenge them. This demotivates the salesperson. They feel powerless.

Then the team starts expecting exceptions. But exceptions destroy consistency. And without consistency, culture loses its backbone.

I have learned something painful but important. Policies do not hurt people. Confusion does.

People often forget that vendors are as much a part of our culture as employees. In our industry, your suppliers decide whether you can fulfill orders or not. Most of our biggest breakthroughs were made possible by our vendors' support during difficult times.

I speak regularly with a friend named Himanshu who is also in the industry. Every few days, we talk, joke, and solve problems for each other. These relationships are not transactional. They are emotional. They are human.

Trust is everything when money and credit are involved. And trust builds over small conversations, honest interactions, and timely support.

Many of our vendor relationships were built by my father. They supported him. And later, they supported me. That loyalty became part of our culture. It helped us grow.

My family is not deeply involved in operations, but their emotional support keeps me going. I work almost eighteen hours a day. I barely get four to five hours of sleep. Without their understanding, none of this would have been possible.

My father and brother are involved in the business, and their presence gives me strength. Even my nephew is now part of the company. When trustworthy family members are honest, it creates stability and direction.

For a long time, we had no HR team. No formal tools. No structured training. Yet people stayed. Why? Because we communicated directly. One to one. With honesty.

We kept a box in the office where anyone could drop their problems confidentially. I personally ensured those issues were resolved. Even today, no matter how large the team becomes, the culture remains personal.

Everyone has a story. And sometimes, listening to that story is enough to create loyalty.

When a new person joins, we do not assume they know anything. We start from zero. We train them in the work, the environment, the process, technology, and the real problems we have faced. We prepare them before they start. Not after.

It is our responsibility to make sure they are ready. And when we do that, they grow faster and better.

In our office, we play cricket. It sounds funny, but one of my hiring questions is: Do you play cricket? Man or woman, it does not matter. I ask everyone. Because cricket creates bonding, joy, and team spirit.

We celebrate birthdays, occasions, festivals, and small moments. These little things build emotional connection.

Not every reward has to be monetary. Sometimes appreciation is about involvement. When I involve people in strategic discussions, they feel valued. They feel seen. They feel trusted.

After office hours, I spend time with employees. We talk freely. They guide me. I guide them. This openness becomes culture.

During office hours, I act as a mentor. After office hours, I act as a family member. People message me anytime. They know I am available. They know I listen. That balance helps the culture grow.

On difficult days, I listen to motivational music, watch startup movies, or read books. They remind me that everyone has problems. Everyone struggles. This helps me stay calm and continue leading.

I would choose people who are mentally strong, visionary, and clear about their growth. People who think beyond their city. People who want to improve every day. People who are psychologically stable and emotionally mature. These qualities matter more than experience.

When I started modernizing the shop, I did not expect resistance from old employees. They were used to traditional systems. When new processes came, they resisted. Some even behaved rudely.

Modernization exposed gaps. People who looked busy were actually not productive. And this created insecurity. We faced politics, negativity, and behavior that slowed the company down. It was one of the hardest phases of my journey.

Whenever there is conflict, I use data. If the data supports the argument, I accept it. If not, we move on. This applies to employees, vendors, and anyone else. Logic reduces arguments. Data ends the drama.

Many times, I misunderstood enthusiastic employees as demotivated. When I realized my mistake, I apologized. I spoke to them personally. I took them out for dinner. I rebuilt trust. Leaders make mistakes, too. What matters is whether we correct them.

Key Takeaways

- Moving from instinct to data changed the way I made decisions.
  Early failures in building systems taught me that resistance often comes from fear, not from flaws.

- Delegation was one of the biggest shifts in my leadership; it freed me from doing everything myself.

- I moved from operator to architect, and the business started scaling only when I stepped back.

- I understood that systems are the true engine behind growth, accountability, and consistency.

Chapter 8

The Silent Battles of the Second Generation

People often assume that inheriting a running business is a blessing. They think it is a shortcut to success, a comfortable path, a ready-made platform. They picture a golden staircase already built, waiting for the next person to climb. What they rarely see is the weight that comes with that staircase. The expectations. The comparisons. The doubts. The internal contradictions. The guilt. The pressure to prove yourself every single day.

For me, being a second-generation entrepreneur has never been a simple story of privilege. It has been a story of identity, insecurity, ambition, and constant self-examination. It has been a journey where I have had to balance gratitude with frustration, legacy with individuality, and responsibility with my own dreams. It has been less about inheriting a business and more about inheriting a battlefield where the biggest fights happen quietly inside my mind.

When people told me I was lucky to inherit a running business, I often laughed from the inside. On the surface, I smiled politely. But inside, the laughter came from a very different place. I felt lucky in a way that people around me never understood. I did not feel lucky because I had a business ready for me. I felt lucky because I got the chance to start from what I call the negative. I entered a business that needed to be rebuilt, rethought, and reimagined.

That, to me, was luck. Luck is when you get a platform that ninety-nine percent of the world would not want. A platform full of chaos, unpredictability, and outdated structures. A platform that needed vision, courage, and reinvention. That was the real gift I got. Not a polished legacy. Not a gold-plated name. Just a foundation that needed rebuilding.

It surprised people when I said I felt lucky. But I meant it. I got something raw. Something complicated. Something imperfect. That is what gave me space to create something of my own. And that feeling still drives me today.

Was I Babysitting a Legacy or Building My Own?

People sometimes assume that second-generation entrepreneurs simply maintain what already exists. Babysit. Preserve. Protect. Keep things running the same way. But from the very beginning, that was never my role. The business I stepped into was not the same business my father had built. It was connected, yes, but only vertically. It was an extension, not a continuation.

I started with a very small shop. A seed. A corner. A starting point. I had to treat it like my own venture because, in reality, it was. I was not babysitting anything. I was building. I was experimenting. I was taking risks. I was responsible for the growth, the direction, and the structure.

The legacy existed emotionally. But what I was building was fundamentally new. It needed a fresh mindset, a different strategy, and a redefined identity. That blend of old foundation and new ambition created a path that felt as much mine as anyone's.

I can name the exact night when I could not sleep because a thought hit me so strongly that it shook my entire sense of time.

It was around 2021 when I saw GoMechanic become a multi-million-dollar company within just four years. I had started before them, at a smaller level, with smaller resources. I remember lying awake, thinking, *"These people are doing this so fast."* They are achieving things at a speed that leaves no space for comfort.

That night awakened something in me. Call it ego, self-respect, or ambition. I started comparing myself not to local businesses or even to people in my circle, but to the world's top leaders. Reliance. Tesla. Maersk. People who build empires with the same twenty-four hours that I have. I told myself, if they can do it, why can't I? They are human beings. I am a human being. The only difference is in how they use their hours and make their decisions.

That night was a turning point. I realized that I had been thinking too small. I was playing a game without knowing the size of the field. And once you realize the size of the field, you can never go back to playing the small game again. That night was the beginning of a new version of me.

Sometimes, in very rare moments, the question does cross my mind. Am I earning this or inheriting this? But the feeling is brief. Almost negligible. Because deep down, I know that we have not even achieved success yet. For me, success will be the IPO. That is the moment I will allow myself to say I built something. Until then, I do not feel I have done anything worth celebrating.

People assume we are already successful because they look at the branches, the growth, the branding, the evolution. But success cannot be measured by external markers. It has to be defined by a milestone you commit to. For me, that milestone is not here yet.

My father had dreams for the business. Big dreams. Whenever he spoke about other industrialists, he admired their ability to create something large, respected, and global. I saw that in him. That dream stayed in my mind like a seed.

But I also had my own dreams. I wanted to build something modern, fast-paced, scalable, and digitally integrated. I wanted a business that could stand globally. I wanted a company that reflected my style, thinking, systems, and philosophy.

So, my journey became a mix. Not just carrying forward what my father dreamed of, but also shaping my own vision. A mix and match of two generations, two styles, and two ambitions.

Yes, society misunderstands second-generation entrepreneurs. People believe everything is served on a platter. They assume you get resources easily. They assume your path is smooth because someone before you laid it down.

But that belief is harmful. It stops young people from joining their family businesses. It pushes them away from opportunities that could be life-changing. It makes them chase something from zero, even when something valuable is waiting for them.

In India, this myth is especially dangerous. Many people lose years trying to build something new when they could have evolved something already built. I believe society needs to understand that inheriting a base is not a shortcut. It is a responsibility. A weight. A challenge. And sometimes a far more complex path.

The Pleasure That Comes from Being Challenged

There is an internal pleasure that drives me almost every day. I feel alive when people challenge me. When they question me. When they doubt me. Whether it is employees, vendors, customers, or even relatives, the moment someone questions my ability, something inside me becomes sharper.

I have always been an insecure person. I do not say that negatively. My insecurity pushes me to improve. It keeps me alert. It makes me ambitious. I thrive when people provoke me or underestimate me.

It becomes fuel. Not the sweet kind. The negative kind. I love proving people wrong. I love answering them with my work. My bat, as I call it. And in my story, work is the bat. Work speaks louder than arguments ever can.

When I speak with my friends or peers, I quickly realize something. Many of them are satisfied with what they have. They have their comfort zones. They have their pace. They have their own definitions of enough.

My mind does not work like that. I am always restless. I am always thinking of something more. Something different. Something better. That is why my conversations sometimes feel mismatched. I look for forward-thinking energy. Future-oriented thinking. Ambition that scares me a little. That is the environment where I thrive.

It is not about comparison. It is about mindset. My vision is simply different from what many of my peers chase.

People often imagine a dramatic moment when a child steps into their parents' shoes. For me, it was not that emotional. My father and I work together even today. We work the same hours. We work on the same shop floor. We fill our own shoes, not each other's.

I never tried to replace him. I could never copy him. He has his style. I have mine. Just like one day my son will fill his own shoes. Generations do not replace each other. They expand each other.

When People Questioned My Capability

Yes, people questioned me openly. Customers, vendors, employees, outsiders. Many of them believed I knew nothing. They assumed I was acting confident without substance. They questioned every new idea, every change, every system I introduced.

Some even told me to slow down because they believed I had learned everything from somewhere else.

I used to smile from the inside when it happened. Every question, every doubt, every sarcastic comment gave me energy. I took it as a personal challenge. Instead of arguing, I strengthened my work. Instead of explaining, I built systems that would speak for themselves.

In many ways, yes. They get respect because the assumption is clear. They built everything from scratch. Their story is romanticized. But I was welcomed by them too. They treated me with respect once they saw how I worked. But in the early days, peers who started from scratch struggled to accept my fast pace and forward thinking. They were comfortable with their rhythm. I was not.

This mismatch pushed me to hire young people. People who wanted change. People who wanted to grow fast. People who were open to new ways. Many of those early recruits are still with me. They shaped the company's foundation. They trusted me even when the older generation doubted me.

People questioned whether I had real authority or whether I was just a figurehead. But authority never came from a title. It came from knowledge, from data, from clarity.

I believe strongly that data is power. Big minds or small minds, it is data that wins the argument. I learned the importance of maths much later in my career. But once I understood it, I realized that numbers give you confidence. They give you the right to challenge any mind in the room.

Identity Conflict: When I Asked Myself Why I Was Doing This

I remember the early days when customers or older people in the ecosystem spoke to me dismissively. They treated me as inexperienced. They demanded things without respect. They underestimated the systems I was trying to build.

In those moments, I wondered why I had to prove myself to anyone. I had studied in good institutions. I had been recruited into good companies. I had promising opportunities. Yet here I was, working at the ground level, convincing people who did not understand where we were headed.

That mismatch created an identity conflict. But slowly, I adapted. I accepted that this was my path. And I learned to treat the discomfort as part of the journey. Yes, I have had five or six moments when I felt I had lost myself in someone else's dream. I questioned whether I had sacrificed my own ambitions. Whether I should have chosen something different. Something faster. Something more aligned with my personality.

I love speed. I love change. I love building things quickly. And sometimes the slow pace of legacy work made me wonder if I was doing the right thing. Those moments were emotionally heavy. But over time, I realized that my speed would shape the business, not the other way around.

People assume I inherited a clear legacy. But there was none. Not in the way people imagine. Yes, I came from a business environment, but when I came to Gurgaon, I started my own venture. The path I was building was not inherited. It was created. The foundation was emotional, not structural.

How My Sense of Work Evolved

Over time, I realized something important. Pressure comes to those who are privileged. It sounds strange, but it is true. If you are trusted with responsibility, pressure will follow.

I work in a segment that is unorganized, unpredictable, and constantly shifting. Nothing comes with instruction manuals. You learn by staying. And staying is an achievement in itself. Many people quit. Many people break. Many people run. But staying, evolving, and adapting is where pride grows. I evolve every day. Every day brings a new challenge and a new version of me.

People think burnout only happens when the business is collapsing. But burnout can happen even when everything looks stable. For me, stability is an illusion. I never believed business is stable. I never believed it in the past, and I never will.

When I feel burnout, I release it through music or cricket. I speak to friends who understand my mindset. I look for active ways to reset myself. I accept that stability does not exist in business, and that acceptance itself keeps me grounded.

Yes, I have felt guilty many times. I have had to be harsh to employees, strict with customers, and firm with processes. These decisions are necessary for the company. But sometimes they go against my personal ethics. And that creates guilt.

Leadership is not about what you personally feel is right. It is about what the company needs. That realization came late. But once it came, I understood why leadership feels heavy even when the business is doing well.

From the outside, growth looks impressive. Branches open. Numbers rise. Systems improve. But I see the gaps internally. I see cracks that others do not. I worry about the long-term implications. I see the risks that could disturb the future.

These unseen gaps create anxiety. It feels like living in two worlds. The world outside sees progress. And the world inside sees what still needs fixing.

I was born with a mindset that enjoys carrying responsibility. Whether it is my family, my employees, or even strangers who depend on me, I feel comfortable holding weight.

People question leadership all the time. They question decisions. They question direction. They question ambition. But leadership is not about pleasing people. It is about holding responsibility even when people do not agree with you.

A Family Moment That Shaped Everything

There was one moment that still stays with me. I had gotten a job outside Delhi. I was promoted within six months. Just before I was supposed to leave, a very close family member told me something I will never forget. He said, if you do not build the foundation now, it will never be built later.

He is not alive today. But that sentence changed my life. It became an anchor. A reminder of the duty I carried.

My breakthrough came on 17 February 2021 when we incorporated the company. That date marks the moment I knew I could shape the business. I believed in my ability. I believed that if others could build something large, I could too.

Ever since that day, every decision has been about shaping, reshaping, and strengthening the path.

I cannot fully describe it, but I feel great pride during struggles. When the struggle is happening, it feels painful. But inside, I know that struggle is guiding me forward. Those moments remind me that growth is happening even before the results appear.

The meaning of success changes for me every day. As I evolve, the definition evolves. At one stage, success was about opening branches. Then it became about building a brand. Now it is about reaching the IPO.

That is my ultimate goal. That is what I see as success today.

Yes. Society judges second-generation entrepreneurs unfairly. People see the platform, not the effort.

They assume shortcuts exist when they do not. We built from scratch in many ways. But people do not see the middle ground. We are not a startup. Neither are we a traditional business. We live in the uncomfortable middle where expectations are high from both sides.

Key Takeaways

- Firefighting had once made me feel important, but I soon realized it was only masking deeper issues.

- Clearly defining roles created structure, ownership, and measurable performance.

- For the first time, I built a five-year vision, and it transformed the way I made decisions.

- Strategy filtered out distractions and gave direction to every aspect of the company.

- The business started running without my constant presence, and that became the true sign of progress.

CHAPTER 9

From Survival to Strategy What Really Matters

FOR THE LONGEST TIME, I believed speed was progress. If I was moving fast, firefighting, fixing things, chasing numbers, and solving problems the moment they appeared, I thought I was growing. It took me years to realize something uncomfortable. I was not building a business. I was surviving it.

Survival mode does not start suddenly. It starts with a small compromise. You skip documenting a process because you are in a rush. You hire the quickest available person instead of the right one because work needs to be done. You handle tasks yourself because training feels slower. You stay in the shop longer, work harder, push more, because it feels easier than creating structure.

Slowly, the habit forms. You begin to believe that your business needs you for everything. That nothing can move without your involvement. That speed is the only way to stay ahead. You are constantly reacting, constantly moving, constantly doing. It feels productive, but the truth is different. You are not growing. You are coping.

I lived this phase deeply. Every day I walked into the business thinking the same thing: *"What needs to be fixed today?"* Not *"What needs to be built?"* There is a huge difference between the two.

Fixing puts you in motion. Building puts you in the direction.

The business was expanding, customers were increasing, revenue was rising, but the foundation was shaky. Growth looked exciting from the outside, but inside, I knew I was one wrong decision or one staff resignation away from chaos. This is the reality of survival-led businesses. They survive, but they never scale.

The Illusion of Busyness

Busyness can feel like purpose. When your phone keeps ringing, when staff are constantly asking questions, and when you are involved in every conversation, you feel important. You feel necessary. You feel productive. I felt that for years. From the outside, I looked like a man in control. Inside, I was a man drowning under the weight of things that should not even have been on my plate.

Coming from a shopkeeper background makes busyness feel normal. Shopkeeping culture celebrates hustle. You open early, close late, attend every customer, negotiate every deal, and track every rupee. Hustle becomes identity. If you are not hustling, you start feeling guilty. You think you are not doing enough.

But hustle has limits. Hustle does not build institutions. Hustle does not build teams. Hustle does not build brands. Hustle only builds dependency. I realized that the more I hustled, the more I became the bottleneck. The team waited for me. Vendors waited for me. Customers waited for me. The business ran on my speed instead of its own systems.

This is the most dangerous illusion in business: thinking that the more you do, the stronger your business becomes. The truth is the opposite. The more dependent the business is on you, the weaker it actually is.

Every transformation has a trigger. Mine came during a period when things were growing too fast for comfort. Sales were rising.

Customer expectations were rising. Staff requirements were rising. Inventory was expanding. Processes were breaking silently in the background. As I handled everything, a strange realization hit me. The business was moving, but I was standing still. There was no long-term planning. No clarity on where the company should be in five years. No defined roles for the team. No documented workflows. Everything lived in my head.

The most painful part was this: I had no time to think.

Constant doing kills clarity. When you are always reacting, you never reflect. When you never reflect, you repeat the same mistakes in new packaging. At one point, I asked myself a question that changed everything. *"If I continue working like this, will this business ever run without me?"*

The answer was no. And if the answer is no, then you are not building a company. You are building a cage. The biggest shift was changing how I saw the business. For years, I saw it as a shop. A shopkeeper's son automatically adopts the mindset of a shop. You see transactions, daily targets, stock levels, customer flow, and everyday issues. You become wired to think in days. But businesses need to think in decades.

A company has departments. A shop has people.

A company has a structure. A shop has habits.

A company has systems. A shop has memory.

A company grows by design. A shop grows by chance.

The moment I understood this difference, everything changed. I stopped treating the business like a shop that needed to move fast. I began treating it like a company that needed clarity. This mindset shift was not one decision. It was a series of small decisions, layered over months, reinforced through trial, error, frustration, arguments, resistance, and breakthroughs.

The Power of Saying No

One of the biggest strategic tools I learned was the power of saying no. A shopkeeper rarely says no. We are trained to say yes to every customer, every opportunity, and every requirement because we fear losing business. But saying yes to everything drains time, energy, focus, and resources. It keeps you busy, but not effective.

Strategy requires refusal. Not every customer is your customer. Not every idea is worth implementing. Not every opportunity deserves your attention. Strategy is not choosing what to do. Strategy is choosing what not to do.

When we stopped taking on certain types of inventories, said no to unprofitable segments, and declined certain vendor attachments, our focus sharpened. Profitability increased. Inventory clarity improved. Customer expectations became simpler. This taught me something profound: Every no strengthens your yes.

If everything is important, nothing is important. This became the central lesson of my transition from survival to strategy. I had to identify the factors that would determine the company's future. Not the fires that appeared daily, but the pillars that would define the next decade.

For me, these pillars were clear:

1. Systems that replaced memory

2. People who could run functions independently

3. Technology that brought visibility and data

4. Branding that built long-term trust

5. Decision-making filters

6. Defined roles and accountability

7. Saying no to things that distracted us. These were not urgent tasks. They were important tasks. Urgent tasks keep you alive. Important tasks help you grow.

Once I understood what mattered, I had to slow down. It sounds counterintuitive, but sometimes slowing down is the fastest way forward. I stopped running behind everything. I stopped picking up every problem. I stopped being the hero who solved everything.

Instead, I started building systems that solved problems before they reached me. I started hiring people who were better than me in certain areas. I started creating documentation so that mistakes would not be repeated. I started delegating not the work I disliked, but the work that could be performed better by someone else.

Direction beats speed.

Clarity beats hustle.

Consistency beats intensity.

This shift brought stability. Stability brought confidence. Confidence brought scale.

Survival mode is impatient. It wants results today. Strategy is patient. It thinks in quarters, not days. This patience was my biggest challenge. For a shopkeeper's mindset, patience looks like inactivity. It feels like laziness. It feels like you are not doing enough.

But patience is not inactivity. Patience is preparation. When we invested time in SOPs, training, documentation, inventory mapping, system testing, realigning departments, and creating processes, nothing looked glamorous. People could not see the value immediately. But long-term structure needs a foundation. Foundation takes time.

Strategy is slow in the beginning and fast in the end. Survival is fast in the beginning and slow in the end.

Breaking the Attachment to Firefighting

Firefighting is addictive. It gives you adrenaline. You feel important. You feel needed. But in strategy-led companies, firefighting is a symptom of system failure, not a sign of dedication.

When I stopped firefighting, people were confused. They brought problems to me. I did not solve them. I redirected them. I asked questions. I pushed them to think. I empowered them to make decisions within clear boundaries.

Slowly, something beautiful happened. People became problem solvers. They stopped running to me for everything. They owned their roles. They took accountability. With every task they took up, I got one minute of my life back. Those minutes added up.

This is what strategy does. It does not make you irrelevant. It makes you irreplaceable.

The Importance of Defining Roles Clearly

Traditional businesses run on habits. People do whatever is needed because that is how they have always worked. Roles are vague. Responsibilities overlap. Accountability disappears.

To shift from survival to strategy, roles had to be clearly defined. Expectations had to be written. Responsibilities had to be measurable. People had to know what success in their role looked like.

Once we defined roles, three things happened:

1. People understood their purpose

2. Confusion was reduced dramatically

3. Performance became visible and measurable

Clarity creates confidence. Confidence creates independence. Independence creates scale.

The Strength of Long-Term Vision

For years, I lacked a long-term vision. I had short-term goals. Revenue targets. Daily sales. Weekly problems. Monthly budgets. But no vision beyond survival.

The first time I sat down and defined a five-year vision, it felt strange. It felt unrealistic. But when we put numbers, structure, and outcomes behind that vision, it suddenly became practical.

Vision creates direction.

Direction creates alignment.

Alignment creates growth.

When you know where you want to go, you make different decisions. You invest differently. You hire differently. You build differently. You say no differently.

The Filters That Changed Everything

Not every decision in a company deserves your time, energy, or attention. Strategic businesses use filters. These are questions that help you evaluate decisions.

My decision filters became:

1. Does this align with our five-year vision?

2. Will this reduce dependency on people?

3. Will this improve customer experience sustainably?

4. Is this profitable long-term?

5. Is this scalable?

6. Is this distracting us from the main direction?

Once these filters became part of our process, decision-making became structured. We took fewer decisions, but better ones.

The final test of strategy is simple. If you are not in the business for one day, does the business stop? If the answer is yes, you are still surviving. If the answer is no, you are building.

Today, the company runs even when I am not physically present. Not perfectly, but independently. That independence did not come from luck. It came from moving away from survival and embracing strategy.

This shift did not just grow the company. It grew me as a leader.

Key Takeaways

- The shop taught me every aspect of business, finance, operations, negotiation, and customer experience, all at once.

- Ground reality gave me urgency, humility, and execution skills no corporate job could have taught.

- When I spoke to investors, my depth came from lived experience, not from presentations.

- I stopped seeing Dukaandaari as something small; I began seeing it as my biggest competitive edge.

- Pride replaced the embarrassment I once felt, because I finally understood the strength that comes from staying power.

CHAPTER 10

Why This Book was Written

PEOPLE OFTEN SAY THAT a book begins with an idea. A spark. A concept. A question that demands exploration. But for me, none of that was true. My book did not begin with a grand vision or a well-defined outline. It began with something much quieter, much more personal, and much more difficult to describe. It began with a feeling.

It was the feeling that something inside me needed space. Not physical space. Emotional space. Mental space. Space to breathe. For years, I had carried thoughts that never found a place to rest. Thoughts that appeared in moments of stress, flashed during moments of growth, and whispered during moments of silence. They were thoughts that I had lived with, but never expressed. They floated around inside me, unorganized, unspoken, unarticulated. And slowly, they became heavy.

It was also the feeling that my journey needed a home. Not a stage, not an audience, not applause. Just a home. A place where my thoughts could sit without fear of being misunderstood. A place where the messy, complicated, unfiltered realities of building something could exist without judgment. I was speaking to hundreds of people every week through my work, but not to myself. This book became the space where I could finally hear myself clearly.

There were countless moments in my life where I tried to express what I felt but could not find the right words.

In conversations, I often held back. Not because I was hiding anything, but because some thoughts felt too raw to share verbally. Some emotions felt incomplete when spoken aloud. Writing gave me the chance to shape them. To understand them. To honor them.

People think that writing is a process of telling. In reality, writing is a process of discovering. When I began putting down the first few lines, I realized how many thoughts I had been carrying without naming them. Thoughts about identity, responsibility, pressure, decisions, legacy, tradition, modernity, confusion, confidence, and growth. These thoughts became clearer when written. They became more honest. They became more real.

The feeling that pushed me to write was not about achievement. It was about honesty. I was not documenting a perfect journey. There was nothing perfect about it. My story had mistakes, failures, delays, doubts, conflicts, and emotions I rarely allowed myself to speak about. But it also had resilience, breakthroughs, clarity, and transformation. Writing allowed me to hold both truths simultaneously.

I did not want to write a book to impress anyone. I wanted to write it to express myself. To take the parts of my life that I had lived internally and bring them into the light. To take the moments that shaped me and give them words. To take the lessons that came through difficulty and make them visible. To take the invisible journey and make it tangible.

The feeling was also about responsibility. Not responsibility to others, but responsibility to myself. I realized that if I did not document this phase of my life, it would slip away silently. I would move on to the next chapter without understanding the one I had just lived. Writing forced me to pause. To reflect. To analyze. To confront. To appreciate. It made me see the journey not as a blur of events, but as a sequence of lessons that built me.

Another part of the feeling was a sense of connection. Deep down, I knew that I was not the only one facing these struggles. There are thousands of people who feel the weight of expectations. Thousands who start their journey unsure, hesitant, or afraid. Thousands who carry stories but never speak them because they think those stories are too ordinary or too imperfect. I wanted this book to become a voice for the quiet battles that so many of us fight alone.

I felt that if my journey could help even one person feel understood, less alone, or more capable, then the vulnerability of writing was worth it. Sometimes, sharing your story gives someone else the courage to start theirs.

Most importantly, the feeling came from an internal need to reconnect with myself. Business can be loud. Growth can be chaotic. Leadership can be overwhelming. In that noise, you lose the softness of your own thoughts. Writing brought me back to them. Writing reminded me of who I was becoming. Writing helped me see the distance between the person I was and the person I wanted to be.

The first words I wrote were not confident. They were not polished. They were not planned. They were honest. And honesty became the foundation of this book.

People assume that books begin with clarity. Mine began with confusion. People assume books begin with inspiration. Mine began with introspection. People assume books begin with ambition. Mine began with vulnerability.

The Spark That Started It

The idea of writing this book did not come from inspiration. It came from pressure. Not pressure from people, but pressure from within. I had years of unspoken thoughts. Years of unanswered questions. Years of experience I had never expressed.

For a long time, I felt those thoughts were scattered, incomplete, or too raw to say aloud. But they stayed with me.

One day, I realized something. If I did not express them, they would remain inside me forever, undefined and unprocessed. Putting them on paper was the only way to give shape to the confusion. This book became a place where I could finally speak without hesitation. A place where my thoughts could stand without defense. A place where I could be honest with myself first, and with the world second.

I began writing not because I had a story to tell, but because I had a story to understand.

And I knew something else. If these thoughts could help me find clarity, they could also help people like me who struggle silently. People who face pressure, expectations, mistakes, failures, fear, and growth at the same time. People who are building their life while building their identity.

This book is for them. And it is for me.

When I started writing, I asked myself a simple question. Is this book only for me, or is it meant for others? The truth is that it was always both.

I wanted to create something that reflected my own journey. A place where I could revisit the mistakes I made, the lessons I learned, and the moments that shaped me. But at the same time, I knew that the things I was writing were universal. The tension between tradition and modernity. The pressure of expectations. The uncertainty of decisions. The struggle to build something meaningful. These challenges are not mine alone. Many people face them. Many people live them quietly.

So this book became a personal reflection with a public purpose. My story, but not only my story. My lessons, but not only my lessons. A personal diary that turned into a shared roadmap.

People assume that writing a book begins with courage. For me, it began with uncertainty. I was excited, yes. I was proud, yes.

But uncertainty was the strongest emotion. What if I could not articulate my thoughts? What if I could not put the feelings into words? What if the story did not make sense when written down? What if my journey was too incomplete to share?

Writing a book is not about finishing. It is about the beginning. And the beginning felt like stepping into an unknown space.

I was not scared. I was unsure. Unsure of whether my story mattered. Unsure of whether my voice was needed. Unsure of whether I could finish what I had started. But the moment I wrote the first chapter, something shifted. I realized that expressing even one part of my journey gave me the strength to express the next.

Clarity does not come before writing. Clarity comes because of writing.

Every chapter came with a challenge. I was running a business while writing a book. That alone created enough conflict. I had to manage growth, handle problems, guide the team, make decisions, run operations, and still find time to write or speak for the book. There were days when it felt impossible.

There were moments when I thought of stopping. Not because I doubted the book, but because I doubted myself. Time was limited. Energy was limited. Mental space was limited. Writing requires emotional honesty, and emotional honesty is difficult to access when you are constantly solving problems in the real world.

But one thought kept me going. If this book could change even one person's life, if it could inspire even one person to stay, build, push, or believe, then the effort was worth it.

This book is not written with the intention to impress. It is written with the intention to impact.

People ask me why I decided to write the book now. The answer is simple. Because Chapter 1 of my life was complete.

Not the entire journey. Not the final achievement. Just Chapter 1. The foundation. The struggles. The transition. The building phase. I felt that this part of my story was ready to be told. The next chapters of my life could only begin once the earlier ones were expressed, understood, and recorded.

Writing this book was a form of closure. And a form of beginning.

The Hesitations I Had

Many people hesitate before telling their story. They fear judgment. They fear misunderstanding. They fear vulnerability. Surprisingly, I did not.

I always wanted to be transparent about my journey. I wanted to show the world not only what I achieved, but what I faced. What I felt. What I struggled with. I did not worry about how family, employees, or peers would perceive my honesty. I believe that openness is a strength. If I could speak my truth, I could stand by it.

The only hesitation I had was whether I would be able to express everything authentically. Whether I could put my real emotions into writing without diluting them. That was the challenge, not fear of judgment.

And what helped me overcome any small hesitation I had was my work. My results. I have always believed that when you do meaningful work, when you are growing, when you are building something real, the fear of being judged disappears. People judge you only when they can see you. And if they can see you, it means you are visible. And if you are visible, it means you are moving.

Being judged is a sign of progress.

When I look back, the hardest part of writing this book was writing about why I decided to write it. Not because I was confused, but because it forced me to confront emotions I had ignored for years.

Speaking about growth is easy. Speaking about struggle is difficult. Speaking about identity, pressure, loneliness, and purpose requires courage. Writing about the early days of my life, the tiffs, the challenges, the internal battles, the moments I never shared with anyone, was emotionally heavy. I have a full family, but I rarely speak about my emotional side. Not because I want to hide it, but because I am not used to sharing it. Writing forced me to open doors inside me that I had kept shut for years.

This book asked me to express things I never expressed anywhere else. That was the hardest part. And the most healing part.

The Flashbacks That Came with Writing

Writing this book was not just writing. It was reliving. Every chapter brought memories I had forgotten or avoided. The old shop. The early customers. The moments of humiliation. The moments of pride. The times when employees taught me lessons. The mistakes I made. The nights of doubt. The mornings of determination.

Some memories felt like wounds reopening. Some felt like victories returning. Some felt like lessons I needed to relearn. But every flashback reminded me why this journey mattered.

We cannot move forward unless we understand where we came from. This book helped me understand.

One of the biggest surprises during this writing journey was the clarity I gained. When I articulated thoughts about data, planning, structure, mistakes, and long-term vision, something clicked. I realized that the clarity I was expressing in the book was the clarity I needed in my business. Writing made me sharper. It made me aware of the gaps between what I was doing and what I wanted to do. It helped me reconnect my actions with my aspirations. It showed me the alignment between my journey and my purpose.

If you want clarity in life, write. Writing forces you to think clearly.

The proudest moments were not achievements. They were in a relationship. The moment my father and I worked as a team. The moment my elder brother joined. The moment my nephew came in. The moment employees brought their families into the company, because they trusted the culture. The moment people believed that the vision was bigger than any one person.

Those moments reminded me that building a business is not about revenue. It is about relationships. It is about creating a place where families grow, not just profits.

This book helped me revisit those memories with gratitude.

There were low points, too. Writing forced me to revisit the tiffs, the loneliness, the emotional burden that I never shared with anyone. I realized how many moments I had kept to myself. Not because I did not trust people, but because I never practiced speaking emotionally.

Writing is difficult when you are honest. But honesty is necessary.

Every time I wrote something painful, I reminded myself that someone reading it might feel less alone. That made the discomfort worth it.

One of the most surprising things was the feedback I received from people who read parts of my journey. They said they could see their own stories in mine, and that they felt understood. That they felt motivated. That they felt less afraid. That they felt like they could also build, even if their beginning was small.

Some people who left us in the early phase returned later and told me that the company's growth gave them hope. They said that our development helped them broaden their vision for their lives. That feedback showed me the real power of storytelling.

Stories connect. Stories influence. Stories lift others.

The Conversations That Stayed with Me

One of the most meaningful conversations was with an early employee named Pradeep. He once said, *"Seeing you gave me the confidence that I can achieve something."* His words stayed with me. Because leadership is not only about guiding people. Leadership is about enabling them to believe in their own future.

Another moment was when my elder brother told me, *"Our vision has increased because of your mindset."* That sentence strengthened my belief that growth is contagious. When one person grows, others expand with him.

These moments reminded me that stories do not just reflect reality. They create it.

I am not a complete second-generation entrepreneur. I am not a complete legacy holder either. I stand somewhere in between. My story resonates with people who are trying to build something from scratch. People are trying to expand something their parents started. People who feel stuck between old traditions and new opportunities. People who want to create but are unsure where to start.

This book is not for one category of people. It is for anyone who feels the pull of building something meaningful, even when the world feels uncertain.

Indian entrepreneurship today is fast, unpredictable, competitive, and emotionally heavy. People start with enthusiasm, but give up when results do not come quickly. My journey taught me the importance of staying, even if growth is slow, even if progress is 0.001 percent, even if expansion feels invisible.

Staying is also a form of moving forward. Consistency is growth. Patience is a strategy. And every entrepreneur needs to hear this.

My story reflects both tradition and modern values. Tradition is the foundation. It is where discipline, ethics, and identity come from.

Modern values are the tools. They are systems, data, structure, planning, and technology. Without tradition, buildings fall. Without modernity, buildings would never expand.

This book shows how both coexist.

Writing this book changed the way I see legacy. Legacy is not a business. It is not revenue. It is not a surname. Legacy is something that continues developing even when you are not there. It is something that grows on its own. Something that becomes independent of you.

This mindset changed my life. And my business.

I am proud to have grown through this process. Every day I learned something. Every day, I improved. Every day, I understood myself better.

rowth is not a destination. It is a habit. And I am proud that I developed that habit.

If this book could change just one person, I would want it to reach someone who wants to start something but is afraid. Someone who is confused, hesitant, or unsure. Someone who doubts their own capability. Someone who thinks society will judge them.

If this book helps even one such person move, then it has done its job.

Someday, I want my son to read this, too. And I hope it changes his perspective in a way that helps him build his own journey.

I want them to feel, *"If he can do it, I can do it too."*

I want them to feel hope.

I want them to feel empowered.

I want them to feel responsible.

I want them to feel capable.

And above all, I want them to feel that staying is a form of strength.

I want them to see it as a positive guide. A message that they can build. A reminder that every generation has its struggles. And a belief that consistency and clarity build the strongest foundations.

You will never feel ready. You become ready only after starting. Action precedes readiness. Confidence is built through movement. Whether it is business, writing, or life, the first step is never perfect. But it is necessary.

Start. That is the only rule.

I want them to apply it constructively. To pace themselves. To structure their thoughts. To improve consistently. To reflect deeply. To act with purpose. And to build with clarity.

If someone asked me whether this book is a manual or a mirror, I would say it is a mirror. It shows who I was, who I am, and who I am becoming. It is not a list of instructions. It is a reflection of the truth. And truth is more powerful than advice.

Success never comes easy. Stay to build one.

I wish I had more clarity. More structure. More self-awareness. Writing showed me that clarity does not come from thinking. It comes from expressing. If I had known this earlier, I would have written sooner.

This book is not only my story. It is an invitation. I want others to share their journey, too. When more stories are shared, more people feel seen. More people learn. More people grow. Stories broaden messages. Stories carry forward legacies. Stories change lives.

Everyone has a story worth sharing. Everyone. You only need one person to listen. And even if nobody listens, sharing will give you clarity you never expected.

For me, the next chapter is clear. The IPO. That is the dream. That is the World Cup for an entrepreneur. That is the milestone I want to achieve before writing the second part of my story.

If you have reached this page, I want you to remember one thing. Clarity comes from expressing. Confidence comes from starting. Growth comes from staying.

You do not need a perfect plan. You need a beginning. You do not need all the answers. You need movement. You do not need approval. You need belief.

Start building. Your story is waiting.

Key Takeaways

- This book began with a feeling, a need for space to express thoughts I had carried silently for years.

- Writing helped me understand myself, my decisions, and the journey that shaped me.

- I didn't write to impress; I wrote to impact someone who might be afraid to begin or stay.

- The honesty in these pages gave me clarity I never had before.

- For me, this book marks the completion of Chapter 1 of my life, the foundation before the next chapter begins.

Conclusion

When I began writing this book, I thought I was telling a story about business. Somewhere along the way, I realized I was telling a story about people. People like you and me. People who stood behind counters, sat in cramped offices, woke up early to open shutters, stayed late to count cash, learned more from customers than from classrooms, and carried the weight of decisions that most of the world never saw. People who wanted to build something meaningful, not because they needed fame, but because they wanted to honor what came before them and create what could come after them.

If you have reached this final chapter, it means you stayed with me through the entire journey. You walked through childhood memories, through myths that shaped identity, through disruptions that created fear, through the generational tug-of-war, through the silent battles of second-generation leadership, through strategy, branding, structure, people, and finally through the truth behind why this book exists. And for that, I want to say thank you. Because a story is only complete when someone receives it with an open heart.

When I started writing, I did not know what the conclusion of this book would look like. Maybe because the story is still evolving. Maybe because growth never has a full stop. Or maybe because I did not want this to feel like an ending. I wanted it to feel like a beginning. Your beginning.

The moment where my story steps aside and makes space for yours.

The reason I wrote this book is simple. I wanted to give voice to a journey that countless entrepreneurs across this country have lived quietly for decades. The journey of the dukaandaar. The journey of the second-generation owner. The journey of the local business dreamer. The journey of those who were not celebrated for starting from zero but judged for not starting from zero. The journey of those who did not choose their starting point but chose to make something out of it anyway.

For years, the world celebrated the startup founder, the unicorn builder, the corporate leader, the risk-taking first-generation entrepreneur. And they deserve every bit of that celebration. But very few spoke about the second-generation entrepreneur. Very few spoke about the unique emotional weight of carrying a legacy. Very few spoke about working with fathers who built their dreams in a completely different era. Very few spoke about the guilt of wanting to change things without hurting what was already working. Very few spoke about the fear of not matching the expectations of the generation before or the ambition of the generation ahead. Very few spoke about the loneliness of being in the middle.

This silence made many of us feel alone in our thoughts. But after speaking to so many people like me, I realized something important. We were never alone. We just never had a space where our stories could breathe. This book became that space.

As I wrote each chapter, I revisited moments I had long forgotten. Some made me smile. Some made me pause. Some made me feel grateful. Some made me feel emotional. But all of them reminded me that nothing in a family business happens in isolation. Every decision, every change, every fight, every idea, every risk, every success, and every failure is connected to people.

Our fathers, our mothers, our team members, our customers, our vendors, and yes, even ourselves.

I realized that the real journey of a second-generation entrepreneur is not about proving the world wrong. It is about understanding yourself. It is about finding clarity in chaos. It is about embracing the identity you once resisted. It is about discovering that you are stronger, wiser, and more capable than you ever thought. It is about forgiving yourself for the mistakes you made while learning. It is about appreciating the discipline your parents built, even when you did not understand it. It is about finding your own voice while respecting theirs. It is about becoming the bridge between what was and what can be.

If there is one message I want this conclusion to leave you with, it is this: your journey is valid. Whether you inherited a shop, a factory, a small office, or an idea, your journey matters. Whether you started with a running business or a broken one, your efforts matter. Whether you feel ahead or behind, your pace matters. Whether you were pushed into the business or chose it willingly, your presence matters. Whether you dream of expanding, modernizing, repositioning, or simply sustaining, your intention matters.

You are not less of an entrepreneur because you did not start from zero. You are an entrepreneur because you chose to continue, to grow, to reimagine, to rebuild, to transform, and to stay accountable. That choice is not small. That choice is not easy. That choice is powerful.

In the years ahead, I hope this book becomes a companion. Not a guidebook, not a textbook, not a set of instructions. Just a companion. Something you revisit when you feel stuck. Something you flip through when you feel misunderstood. Something you reread when you need clarity. Something that reminds you that your journey is supposed to challenge you, shape you, stretch you, and strengthen you.

Being a second-generation entrepreneur is not about following in footsteps. It is about expanding them. It is not about filling someone else's shoes. It is about growing into your own. It is not about blindly maintaining tradition. It is about honoring it with evolution. It is not about breaking away from family. It is about creating a future that includes them in a new way. It is not about choosing between dukaandaar and entrepreneur. It is about being both with pride.

If there is one thought I want you to carry forward, it is this: legacy is not a restriction. Legacy is a foundation. And what you build on that foundation is yours alone.

So, step into the future with confidence. Carry your roots with strength. Challenge old habits when necessary. Embrace new systems when useful. Build your brand with honesty. Invest in your people with intention. Make decisions with clarity. And whenever fear whispers in your ear, remember that it whispered to me, too. And I moved anyway. You can too.

This is not the end of the book. This is the beginning of a new chapter in your own story. A chapter that you will write not with certainty, but with courage. Not with comparison, but with clarity. Not with pressure, but with purpose.

Thank you for allowing me to share my journey. Thank you for letting these words become part of your thoughts for a while. Thank you for walking with me from the shop counter to strategy, from confusion to clarity, from expectation to identity.

Now, as you close this book, I invite you to open something else. A notebook. A conversation. A plan. A decision. A dream. Because the world does not need more perfect entrepreneurs. It needs more honest ones. It needs more grounded ones. It needs more courageous ones. It needs more entrepreneurs who build not just businesses, but meaning.

WELCOMES YOU

About the author

Prateek Jain is an entrepreneur whose journey reflects persistence, resilience, and the power of grounded learning. Unlike many entrepreneurs shaped in startup ecosystems, his foundation was built in a small automobile spare parts shop, where his understanding of business developed through real-world exposure rather than formal training alone.

Born and raised in Delhi, Prateek's early lessons in business came from observing his father's work, interacting with customers, managing inventory, negotiating with suppliers, and maintaining discipline in daily operations. These experiences laid the foundation for his entrepreneurial thinking.

He completed his MBA from IMT Nagpur and later pursued executive education at IIM Calcutta. After beginning his career in the corporate world, he chose to leave a stable job in 2016 to join his family's automobile spare parts business. The transition was challenging, as he started from a small shop in Gurgaon, handling every aspect of the business himself.

Between 2016 and 2021, his focus remained on stabilizing the business, building relationships, and understanding the industry at a practical level. In 2021, the business reached an important milestone by breaking even, marking the shift from survival to stability.

In the same year, he formally incorporated the business, taking the first structured step toward transforming a traditional shop into an organized enterprise.

From there, the business expanded into multiple outlets and moved toward a larger vision of building a comprehensive automobile ecosystem. Through his venture, CarTrends, Prateek combines the strengths of traditional trade with modern systems, branding, and scalable business practices.

Prateek is also a strong advocate for changing perceptions around traditional businesses, emphasizing that shopkeepers are entrepreneurs who manage risk, relationships, and responsibility daily.

www.ingramcontent.com/pod-product-compliance
Lightning Source LLC
Chambersburg PA
CBHW020324180726
47991CB00018B/606